WHO MOVED THE STONE?

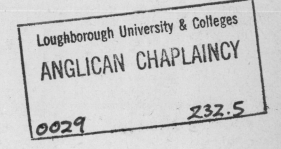

Who Moved the Stone?

by

FRANK MORISON

'. . . Suffered under Pontius Pilate, was crucified, dead, and buried . . . The third day he rose again from the dead . . .'

FABER AND FABER
London · Boston

First published in 1930
by Faber and Faber Limited
3 Queen Square London WC1
First published in this edition 1958
Reprinted 1959, 1962, 1963, 1965,
1967, 1969, 1971, 1972, 1975 and 1978
Printed in Great Britain
by Jarrold and Sons Ltd, Norwich
All rights reserved

ISBN 0 571 03259 1 (Faber Paperbacks)
ISBN 0 571 06929 0 (hard bound edition)

PREFACE

This study is in some ways so unusual and provocative that the writer thinks it desirable to state here very briefly how the book came to take its present form.

In one sense it could have taken no other, for it is essentially a confession, the inner story of a man who originally set out to write one kind of book and found himself compelled by the sheer force of circumstances to write quite another.

It is not that the facts themselves altered, for they are recorded imperishably in the monuments and in the pages of human history. But the interpretation to be put upon the facts underwent a change. Somehow the perspective shifted —not suddenly, as in a flash of insight or inspiration, but slowly, almost imperceptibly, by the very stubbornness of the facts themselves.

The book as it was originally planned was left high and dry, like those Thames barges when the great river goes out to meet the incoming sea. The writer discovered one day that not only could he no longer write the book as he had once conceived it, but that he would not if he could.

To tell the story of that change, and to give the reasons for it, is the main purpose of the following pages.

CONTENTS

Chapter I

THE BOOK THAT REFUSED TO BE WRITTEN

I suppose that most writers will confess to having hidden away somewhere in the secret recesses of their most private drawer the first rough draft of a book which, for one reason or another, will never see the light of day.

Usually it is Time—that hoary offender—who has placed his veto upon the promised task. The rough outline is drawn up in a moment of enthusiasm and exalted vision; it is worked upon for a time and then it is put aside to await that leisured 'tomorrow' which so often never comes. Other and more pressing duties assert themselves; engagements and responsibilities multiply, and the treasured draft sinks further and deeper into its ultimate hiding-place. So the years go by, until one day the writer awakens to the knowledge that, whatever other achievements may be his, this particular book will never be written.

In the present case it was different.

It was not that the inspiration failed, or that the day of leisure never came. It was rather that when it did come the inspiration led in a new and unexpected direction. It was as though a man set out to cross a forest by a familiar and well-beaten track and came out suddenly where he did not expect to come out. The point of entry was the same; it was the point of *emergence* that was different.

Let me try to explain briefly what I mean.

When, as a very young man, I first began seriously to study the life of Christ, I did so with a very definite feeling that, if I may so put it, His history rested upon very insecure foundations.

If you will carry your mind back in imagination to the late

'nineties you will find in the prevailing intellectual attitude of that period the key to much of my thought. It is true that the absurd cult which denied even the historical existence of Jesus had ceased to carry weight. But the work of the Higher Critics—particularly the German critics—had succeeded in spreading a very prevalent impression among students that the particular form in which the narrative of His life and death had come down to us was unreliable, and that one of·the four records was nothing other than a brilliant apologetic written many years, and perhaps many decades, after the first generation had passed away.

Like most other young men, deeply immersed in other things, I had no means of verifying or forming an independent judgment upon these statements, but the fact that almost every word of the Gospels was just then the subject of high wrangling and dispute did very largely colour the thought of the time, and I suppose I could hardly escape its influence.

But there was one aspect of the subject which touched me closely. I had already begun to take a deep interest in physical science, and one did not have to go very far in those days to discover that scientific thought was obstinately and even dogmatically opposed to what are called the miraculous elements in the Gospels. Very often the few things the textual critics had left standing Science proceeded to undermine. Personally I did not attach anything like the same weight to the conclusions of the textual critics that I did to this fundamental matter of the miraculous. It seemed to me that purely documentary criticism might be mistaken, but that the laws of the Universe should go back on themselves in a quite arbitrary and inconsequential manner seemed very improbable. Had not Huxley himself declared in a peculiarly final way that 'miracles do not happen', while Matthew Arnold, with his famous gospel of 'Sweet Reasonableness', had spent a great deal of his time in trying to evolve a non-miraculous Christianity?

For the person of Jesus Christ Himself, however, I had a deep and even reverent regard. He seemed to me an almost legendary figure of purity and noble manhood. A coarse

10

word with regard to Him, or the taking of His name lightly, stung me to the quick. I am only too conscious how far this attitude fell short of the full dogmatic position of Christianity. But it is an honest statement of how at least one young student felt in those early formative years when superficial things so often obscure the deeper and more permanent realities which lie behind.

It was about this time—more for the sake of my own peace of mind than for publication—that I conceived the idea of writing a short monograph on what seemed to me to be the supremely important and critical phase in the life of Christ—the last seven days—though later I came to see that the days immediately succeeding the Crucifixion were quite as crucial. The title I chose was 'Jesus, the Last Phase', a conscious reminiscence of a famous historical study by Lord Rosebery.

I took the last seven days of the life of Jesus for three reasons:

1. This period seemed remarkably free from the miraculous element which on scientific grounds I held suspect.
2. All the Gospel writers devoted much space to this period, and, in the main, were strikingly in agreement.
3. The trial and execution of Jesus was a reverberating historical event, attested indirectly by a thousand political consequences and by a vast literature which grew out of them.

It seemed to me that if I could come at the truth *why* this man died a cruel death at the hands of the Roman Power, how He Himself regarded the matter, and especially how He behaved under the test, I should be very near to the true solution of the problem.

Such, briefly, was the purpose of the book which I had planned. I wanted to take this Last Phase of the life of Jesus, with all its quick and pulsating drama, its sharp, clear-cut background of antiquity, and its tremendous psychological and human interest—to strip it of its overgrowth of primitive beliefs and dogmatic suppositions, and to see this supremely great Person as He really was.

I need not stay to describe here how, fully ten years later, the opportunity came to study the life of Christ as I had long wanted to study it, to investigate the origins of its literature, to sift some of the evidence at first hand, and to form my own judgment on the problem which it presents. I will only say that it effected a revolution in my thought. Things emerged from that old-world story which previously I should have thought impossible. Slowly but very definitely the conviction grew that the drama of those unforgettable weeks of human history was stranger and deeper than it seemed. It was the *strangeness* of many notable things in the story which first arrested and held my interest. It was only later that the irresistible logic of their meaning came into view.

I want to try, in the remaining chapters of this book, to explain why that other venture never came to port, what were the hidden rocks upon which it foundered, and how I landed upon, to me, an unexpected shore.

Chapter II

THE REAL CASE AGAINST THE PRISONER

In attempting to unravel the tangled skein of passions, prejudices, and political intrigues with which the last days of Jesus are interwoven, it has always seemed to me a sound principle to go straight to the heart of the mystery by studying closely the nature of the charge which was brought against Him.

I remember this aspect of the question coming home to me one morning with new and unexpected force. I tried to picture to myself what would happen if some two thousand years hence a great controversy should arise about one who was the centre of a criminal trial, say, in 1922. By that time most of the essential documents would have passed into oblivion. An old faded cutting of *The Times* or *Telegraph*, or perhaps some tattered fragment of a legal book describing the case, might have survived to reach the collection of an antiquary. From these and other fragments the necessary conclusions would have to be drawn. Is it not certain that people living in that far-off day, and desiring to get at the real truth about the man concerned, would go first to the crucial question of the charge on which he was arraigned? They would say: 'What was all the trouble about? What did his accusers say and bring against him?' If, as in the present instance, several charges appear to have been preferred, they would ask what was the *real case* against the prisoner?

Directly we set this question in the forefront of our inquiry, certain things emerge which throw new and unexpected light upon the problem. It will help us to an understanding of what these significant things are if we consider first the very singular character of the trial itself. For not

13

only did it take place at an unprecedented hour for such proceedings, but it was marked throughout by peculiarities of a special kind. Consider in the first instance the vital element of time.

All the historians agree that the arrest of Jesus took place in the Garden of Gethsemane at a late hour on the evening immediately preceding the day of the Crucifixion, and there is strong justification for believing that it could not possibly have been earlier than eleven-thirty.

This estimate is based upon the amount of time required by the recorded events between the breaking up of the Supper Party, probably in a house in the Upper City, and the arrival of the armed band in the garden at the foot of Olivet. There are three things which point irresistibly to the hour being late:

1. The disciples were manifestly tired, and even the sturdy fisherman Peter, accustomed to lonely vigils on the deep, could not keep awake.

2. Both St. Matthew and St. Mark refer to three separate periods of slumber, broken by the periodical return of Christ from His prolonged communing under the neighbouring trees.

3. The fact that it was quite dark, and that owing to the use of torches, Christ was able to discern the approach of the arrest party a considerable distance off (see St. Mark xiv. 42: 'Arise, let us be going: behold, he that betrayeth me is at hand.').

No one can read the records of this extraordinary episode without realizing that this particular sojourn in the garden was different from any of those previous visits to the same spot hinted at by St. John. These men were being held there by the will of Christ long after the time when they would ordinarily have been in their beds at Bethany. They were waiting at His bidding for something for which He also was waiting, and which was an unconscionably long time in coming. Assuming the supper to have been over at nine-thirty and the Garden itself reached so early as 10 p.m., the arrest could hardly have been effected much before eleven-thirty. This fixes for us with some certainty the hour of the preliminary trial.

It is generally agreed by archæologists and students of the

topography of ancient Jerusalem that an old flight of steps descended from the Upper City to the gate leading to the pool of Siloam at the south-eastern angle of the City wall. It is mentioned by Nehemiah (Chap. iii. 15): 'The stairs that go down from the city of David'; and again (Chap. xii. 37): 'By the fountain gate, and straight before them, they went up by the stairs of the city of David, at the going up of the wall.'

There were thus two routes open to the arrest party. One was to follow the course of the Kedron Valley to the foot of these steps, and thence to the High Priest's house. The other was to take the main Bethany road into the new town and thence by the Tyropæan Valley to the Priestly quarter. Even if tradition had not strongly indicated the former, it is clear that to have conducted Jesus through the populous quarter of the Lower City would not only have been inexpedient, but would have necessitated a detour by which valuable time would have been lost. And in this strange nocturnal business time was a very important factor.

If, therefore, by some magic reversal of the centuries we could have stood at some vantage-point in old Jerusalem about midnight or shortly afterwards on that memorable 14 Nizan, we should probably have witnessed a small party of men leading a strangely unresisting figure through the darkness, along the rocky defile which skirted the precipitous eastern face of the Temple wall, up the historic causeway at the south-eastern angle of the City wall to the headquarters of His avowed and inveterate enemies.

How did it come about that the most distinguished Hebrew of His generation found Himself in this dangerous and menacing situation, at the dead of night, on the eve of one of the most solemn of the Jewish Festivals? What were the secret and hidden forces which precipitated His arrest? Why was this particular and highly inconvenient moment chosen? Above all, what was the gravamen of the charge which was brought against Him?

It will require very much more than this chapter to answer these questions, to which indeed the whole book is a very partial and inadequate reply. But there are two things which stand out very sharply from the records of this trial and which call for the closest study. The first is the peculiar nature of the only definite charge which was brought against Jesus. The second is the admission upon which His conviction was based.

Now it seems to me that we shall make a very grievous mistake if we assume (as has so often been done by Christian writers) that everything that the priests did that night was *ultra vires* and illegal. Of course, there are aspects of the affair which, on any reading of the case, must be considered definitely, and even flagrantly, to be at variance with the Jewish Law. That, I think, is conceded by every competent student of the Mischna and of Jewish institutions as they existed at the time.

It was illegal, for example, for the Temple Guard, acting officially as the instrument of the High Priest, to effect the arrest. That should have been left to the voluntary action of the witnesses. It was illegal to try a capital charge (Trial for Life) by night. Only 'trials for money' could be conducted after sunset. It was illegal, after the testimony of the witnesses had broken down, for the judges to cross-examine the Prisoner. They should have acquitted Him, and if the testimony given was demonstrably *false*, the witnesses should have been sentenced to death by stoning.

These things lie upon the surface of the situation. But beneath these flagrant instances of irregularity in the trial of Jesus, there runs a strong undercurrent of legality—an almost meticulous observance of certain minor points of the law—which is very illuminating and instructive to the impartial student of history.

This fact emerges very strikingly if we study the singular way in which the very ground of the accusation shifted during the course of the trial. As everyone who has attentively studied the records knows, there were in all three main charges brought against Jesus during the course of the successive phases of the trial. We may summarize them briefly as follows:

1. That He had threatened to destroy the Temple.
2. That He had claimed to be the Son of God.
3. That He had stirred up the people against Cæsar.

The Real Case Against the Prisoner

The third of these charges can be dismissed from our consideration at once. It was not the real grievance of the Jews. It was framed solely for political ends. The Roman law took no cognizance of the offences for which Christ was condemned to death, yet without Pilate the death could not be consummated. It was absolutely necessary, therefore, to find a political charge to justify before the Roman procurator the extreme penalty which they had already tacitly imposed. They chose the charge of conspiracy against Cæsar because it was the only kind of charge which would carry weight with Pontius Pilate, or indeed with any representative of the Roman Power. Even that almost failed, and would have failed completely, had the procuratorship been in stronger hands.

But, as I have said above, it does not matter what the ostensible charge before Pilate was. The thing we are concerned with very deeply is what the *real* charge of the Jews was against Christ. Directly we concentrate upon this we get an extraordinarily luminous view of what was behind the prosecution.

It must be remembered that, according to a long-established Hebrew custom, the accusers in a Jewish criminal trial were the witnesses. No other form of prosecution was legal, and the first clearly defined act in the midnight drama, after the Prisoner had been brought before the Court, was the calling of witnesses, as the law demanded. Both St. Matthew and St. Mark are quite explicit upon this point.

St. Mark says: 'Many bare false witness against him.'
St. Matthew says: 'Many false witnesses came.'

And St. Mark affirms that the evidence of these witnesses did not 'agree together' and was therefore overthrown.

To those unfamiliar with the subtleties of Jewish jurispridence, and especially with the singular orientation of the law in favour of the prisoner, it may seem curious that, having been at considerable pains to secure witnesses for the prosecution, the Court should have proceeded forthwith to *reject* the evidence. If the story of the witnesses was a deliberate fabrication, it should not have been very difficult to have harmonized it in advance, or, in the ancient phraseology, to have made it 'agree together'. The very fact that the Court did reject the testimony proves that in this fundamental matter of the witnesses even Caiaphas himself was under some compelling necessity to follow the traditional and characteristic Hebrew usage in a 'trial for life'.

What that usage was is described for us with great wealth of detail in the Mischna. There were three classes of testimony recognized by the law:

1. A vain testimony.
2. A standing testimony.
3. An adequate testimony.

Now there was a very practical distinction between these three classes of evidence. A 'vain testimony' was testimony obviously irrelevant or worthless, and immediately recognized by the judges as such. A 'standing testimony' was evidence of a more serious kind to be accepted provisionally, until confirmed or otherwise. An 'adequate testimony' was evidence in which the witnesses 'agreed together'. 'The least discordance between the evidence of witnesses' (says the distinguished Jewish writer, Salvador) 'was held to destroy its value.'

It is clear, therefore, that whatever may have been the subject-matter of the preliminary witnesses referred to by the two Evangelists, it did not get beyond the second and provisional stage. This can only mean that it was either demonstrably contrary to the experience and knowledge of the Court, or it was invalidated on technical grounds. St. Mark's statement that it did not 'agree together' strongly indicates the latter.

But now comes a very curious thing. When this preliminary and unsatisfactory witness had been cleared away, two men came forward with a very definite and circumstantial piece of evidence.

St. Mark says:

'There stood up certain, and bare false witness against him, saying, We heard him say, I will destroy this temple that is made with hands, and in three days I will build another made without hands.'

18

St. Matthew, who in this case is probably not quoting St. Mark, but drawing upon another ancient source, confirms it by saying:

'But afterward came two, and said, This man said, I am able to destroy the temple of God and to build it in three days.'

Whatever else took place, therefore, on that memorable night, it seems certain that two men came forward and, with the torchlight falling full on the face of Christ, accused Him of having used words similar to these. That is a very important fact, and I will ask the reader to keep it in mind for a few moments.

Now the thing of immediate importance is to know whether these men were deliberately inventing the charge or were merely perverting for their own purpose an actual and somewhat similar saying of Christ. Even if no other data were available, I should personally hesitate to believe that so definite and circumstantial a statement was a pure invention. It is a much more deadly thing to distort what a man has said in the hearing of others than to lie deliberately about him. The distortion will elicit uproarious support from overwrought and angry men. Only the most brazen will voice approval of a deliberate and calculated lie. It always has been so, and we can be reasonably sure that it was so in this case. These men had heard Christ make a resounding statement in the Temple courts, and there was no more deadly thing which they could do than to give a distorted and misleading version of it at His trial.

But there is another, and, to me, a very conclusive reason why we may regard the testimony of these witnesses as a reflex of something which Christ Himself actually said on some public occasion. Both men declared that they had heard the Prisoner use certain words which, if substantiated, involved the double offence of sorcery and sacrilege. The penalty for sorcery was death. The penalty for sacrilege was stoning and exposure of the body. From the standpoint of the enemies of Jesus a more fatal charge could hardly have been laid to His account. *Yet still the testimony was overthrown.*

Now why was that? There must be a satisfactory and historical explanation. If the testimony of these two men had been an absolute invention; if it had originated in the scheming brain of Caiaphas, and the witnesses had, so to say, been 'put up' to play their part, there would surely have been no bungling of the affair in this naïve and exasperating way. After all, the witnesses had only a few words to say, and the most elementary sort of prudence should have secured their agreement in advance. The case against Christ ought to have gone swiftly and triumphantly to a conviction.

But we do not find that kind of situation at all. We find a situation in which the Court, despite the illegality of its sitting at this very late hour, wasted a great deal of precious time upon a judicial process which carried it nowhere. At the end of all this elaborate hearing of witnesses Jesus Christ was virtually an unaccused, and certainly an unconvicted man. The entire proceedings threatened to break down upon a vital point of Jewish Law.

Two things emerge from this unquestionably historic fact. In the first place Caiaphas was clearly not all-powerful to work his will in that assembly. There were evidently very strong influences in the Council Chamber in favour of a rigorous observance of the law, particularly in the crucial matter of the witnesses. It must always be remembered that the judgment of this tribunal was not final. Whatever these men did that night had to pass muster the next morning before the Great Sanhedrin in plenary sitting. There had apparently been trouble once before when Nicodemus, a member of that body, had protested against condemnation without a fair hearing. They could justify the illegality of the night hearing of the case on the ground of high political necessity, and the near approach of the Feast. But any serious flaw in the accusation might easily have led to the compulsory release of the Prisoner at a moment when immense multitudes would unquestionably have flocked to His side.

The very fact, too, that the testimony was being sifted so rigorously implies a corresponding cautiousness of statement by the witnesses themselves. Under the Jewish system of jurisprudence, weighted as it undoubtedly was to lean in favour of the accused, it was a very dangerous thing to be a witness in a 'trial for life'. The penalty for uttering a false testimony was death. Hence the number of these trials was few.

But the really impressive inference from all these singular proceedings is surely this: If the testimony was *not* pre-concerted; if its disagreement both surprised and exasperated the high priest, it is clear that it was at least *bona-fide* testimony, and bore some definite relation to the facts. Thus, even if the writer of St. John's Gospel had not preserved for us what we may call the 'official' version of what took place in the Temple courts, we should be compelled to believe that Jesus did upon some historical occasion use some words closely resembling those with which He was charged.

What was the historic utterance which lay behind this charge? What did Jesus really say to give rise to these circumstantial statements? There are three versions from which we may choose. According to St. Mark's 'witness' Jesus deliberately threatened to destroy the Temple and to replace it magically in three days. The words are very explicit:

'I will destroy this temple that is made with hands, and in three days I will build another made without hands.'

St. Matthew's witness modifies and softens the accusation considerably. The suggestion of the magical replacement of the Temple is still there, but Christ is represented as only claiming the *power* to do this:

'This man said, I am able to destroy the temple of God, and to build it in three days.'

Can we, in the absence of a more authentic version of what the original utterance was, accept either of these statements as the true one? Surely we cannot without doing violence to the whole Synoptic impression of the historic Jesus. For consider their import. Jesus is made to say that, of His own power and volition, He could pull down the Temple of Herod, or cause it to fall down, or disappear, and replace it by another. Such a claim could, of course, only be validated

21

by the exercise of supernormal or magical powers beyond anything ever asserted of Christ, and beyond the wildest dreams of the most deluded disciple of Eastern necromancy. Indeed, we may say that no really sane person, especially one of the spiritual and moral category to which Christ belongs, would make a statement of this particular sort.

We can imagine some fanatical and half-witted person, whose whole mentality bordered on the insane, throwing out this preposterous boast in a sudden access of frenzy, knowing full well that he would never be called upon to justify it. But the Prisoner in this trial does not come within that definition. He does not come within a thousand miles of it. In all His story there is no trace of those characteristics which are the hall-mark of the unstable mind. On the other hand, there are many indications of that high sanity which accompanies a firmly disciplined mind. He seems to have been supremely a lover of truth and sincerity, and that inner humility which is man's greatest claim to kinship with God; He was a great hater of shams and hypocrisies and futile boasts. Moreover, He was a somewhat shy and intensely sensitive man. No one with an eye for historic truth, flashing out of the ancient pages of His record, can fail to see what happened when they brought to Him the woman taken in adultery. He *blushed*, and He stooped to write in the sand that He might cover His momentary confusion and regain the moral poise which a public situation attended with peculiarly indelicate and disgusting elements demanded. There, if anywhere, you have a glimpse of the real Jesus of history. It rings true with the memorable moral sayings recorded of Him. But it does not ring true with this grotesque and overweening boast.

The version of two witnesses, therefore, must at least be held suspect until we have corroborative testimony of the most emphatic kind. But the evidence at our disposal points in quite a different direction. According to St. John, what Jesus really did say was: 'Destroy this temple and in three days I will raise it up.' And the writer adds parenthetically: 'But he spake of the temple of his body.'

Of course, no serious student of this problem will deny for

a moment that this is a difficult saying. It is difficult whatever interpretation is put upon it. But if we are to decide between three divergent and contradictory readings, I am bound to say that there is one thing which impresses me profoundly—the fact that *the words 'in three days' are found in them all.* I do not think that the immense weight of that circumstance has been fully realized.

In ordinary life, when confronted with several divergent accounts of a given happening, it is a sound and consistent rule to examine first the points upon which the narrators are agreed. The presumption that such points of agreement represent something solid and original is very strong. Particularly is this the case when the witnesses come, as it were, from opposite camps, and are in marked disagreement upon other essential features of the case.

Now the peculiarity of the phrase 'in three days' lies in the fact that it occurs very rarely in the recorded teaching of Christ, and then only in circumstances which have seemed to many critics to present grave doubts as to the authenticity of the passages in question. Take, for example, the three outstanding instances which occur in the Gospel of St. Mark:

Mark viii. 31: 'And he began to teach them, that the Son of man must suffer many things, and be rejected by the elders, and the chief priests, and the scribes, and be killed, and after three days rise again.'

Mark ix. 31: 'For he taught his disciples, and said unto them, The Son of man is delivered up into the hands of men, and they shall kill him; and when he is killed, after three days he shall rise again.'

Mark x. 33: 'Behold, we go up to Jerusalem; and the Son of man shall be delivered unto the chief priests and the scribes; and they shall condemn him to death, and shall deliver him unto the Gentiles: and they shall mock him, and shall spit upon him, and shall scourge him, and shall kill him; and after three days he shall rise again.'

The modern reader, coming to these passages with a certain instinctive reluctance to accept anything which transcends the field of normal experience is inclined to say: 'I can understand Jesus predicting His own death. He must have foreseen what was the probable outcome of the ever-widening gap between Himself and the priests, and I think it is not unlikely that He may have prepared the disciples privately for the event. But surely these direct references to His rising from the dead can only have been written after His death and are not an integral part of the original utterances.'

Let us admit frankly that it does look like that at first sight. And yet when we come to examine closely the minutes of this trial with all its primitive marks of authenticity; its meticulous and, in the end, fruitless hearing of hostile witnesses; we make the startling discovery that these very words ('in three days') which reason asserts *could never have been uttered by Christ*, are precisely the words which according to all the witnesses formed the pith and core of the fatal and historic sentence with which He was charged. It would have been a strange coincidence indeed if the one sentence chosen by the enemies of Christ upon which to base the most deadly charge they could bring against Him found no counterpart or parallel whatever in all the varied teaching of the two preceding years.

What, then, do we find? We find the Prisoner accused of making a claim so fantastic and absurd that, even if His judges had not rejected the testimony, we should have had to receive it with the gravest possible doubt. Yet from the very texture of the circumstances there seems to emerge the fact that what He probably did say was more extraordinary still.

He said in effect: 'If you kill me, I will rise again from the grave.' I see no escape from the logic of that conclusion. We may hold that He was mistaken; that He was held by some strange mental obsession which periodically flashed out in His public utterance. But that He said this singular and almost unbelievable thing seems to me to be very nearly beyond the possibility of doubt.

*   *   *   *   *

But we have still to consider the other outstanding feature of this remarkable trial. Jesus of Nazareth was condemned to death, not upon the statements of His accusers, but upon an admission extorted from Him under oath.

The Real Case Against the Prisoner

It is clear that after the hearing of the witnesses, and the final rejection of their testimony, the whole conduct of the case began to take an unquestionably illegal form. The illegality consisted in the President of the Court attempting to supply, by direct questioning of the Prisoner, the necessary grounds for a conviction which the witnesses themselves had been unable to produce.

This was, of course, directly contrary both to the letter and the spirit of the elaborate judicial code by which the Jewish Law sought to protect the life of the citizen. The power of accusation in a Hebrew 'trial for life' was vested solely in the witnesses. It was their business to effect the arrest and to bring the accused man to the Court. It was the duty of the Court to protect the interests of the Prisoner in every possible way, while seeking to arrive at a just and impartial judgment on the evidence submitted.

That this judicial protection was not extended to the Prisoner in the present case is clear from even a superficial reading of the narrative. It comes out in the tone of marked exasperation with which the High Priest addressed the Prisoner when the last of the long line of testimonies had broken down.

'Answerest thou nothing? What is it which these witness against thee?'

In itself this question was perhaps not objectionable. As an accused man Christ undoubtedly had the right to bring forward any facts or explanations in His defence. Hitherto He had maintained complete silence. It was appropriate that He should be asked if He had anything to say bearing on the evidence. It is the unveiled hostility to the Prisoner which is so significant, and which instinctively warns us of what is to follow. For, in the next moment, the High Priest seems to have thrown all pretence at legality to the winds.

Standing in his place, in the centre of the tribunal, Caiaphas applied to Christ the most solemn form of oath known to the Hebrew Constitution, the famous Oath of the Testimony. 'I adjure thee by the living God' (Matthew xxvi.

63). To this, Christ, as a pious and law-abiding Jew, had no alternative but to answer.

'If' (says the Mischna) 'one shall say, I adjure you by the Almighty, by Sabaoth, by the Gracious and Merciful, by the Long-suffering, by the Compassionate, or by any of the Divine titles, behold they are bound to answer.'

Stripped of the peculiar phraseology with which the Hebrew mind of the period invested the conception of the Messiah, the question which Caiaphas, the High Priest, put to Jesus was a direct and simple one:

'Art thou the Christ? Dost thou claim to be He that shall come?'

The reply of the Prisoner was not less direct. Here are the three versions:

'I am' (Mark xiv. 62).
'Thou hast said' (Matthew xxvi. 64).
'Ye say that I am' (Luke xxii. 70).

As Mr. Baring Gould has pointed out, these answers are really identical. The formulæ 'Thou hast said' or 'Ye say that I am', which to modern ears sound evasive, had no such connotation to the contemporary Jewish mind. 'Thou sayest' was the traditional form in which a cultivated Jew replied to a question of grave or sad import. Courtesy forbade a direct 'yes' or 'no'.

Christ therefore said this very considerable thing with great definiteness and emphasis. The satisfaction of Caiaphas at obtaining by a single stroke this tremendous and (from the Prisoner's standpoint) very dangerous confession is obvious. One can almost hear the ring of triumph in his voice as he swung round upon the assembled rabbis and exclaimed:

'What further need have we of witnesses? Ye have heard the blasphemy: what think ye?'

Now to the student whose mind is alert for what I may call the *submerged* facts of the story, this sudden rising of the case to its dramatic climax is full of interest.

26

The Real Case Against the Prisoner

Why did the trial suddenly take this pronouncedly unconstitutional form at a relatively late hour in the proceedings, after much valuable time had been occupied in sifting the evidence of the witnesses? If the compulsory affirmation of the Prisoner was sufficient to secure conviction, why were the witnesses heard at all?

The answer to these questions lies undoubtedly in the peculiar nature of the tactical and judicial problem which confronted Caiaphas. That the powerful Sadducean family to which the High Priest belonged had fully determined to get Jesus out of the way is obvious, and nothing but the death penalty would satisfy them. Yet, strangely enough, even an indisputably proven case of blasphemy or sorcery was not sufficient. Caiaphas had to look beyond the purists of the Great Sanhedrin and the provisions of the Mosaic Law to that far more formidable barrier, the power and tolerance of Rome.

None knew better than Caiaphas what were the personal and political consequences of the coming of the real Messiah in the flesh. That it involved some definite kind of Kingship, with Jerusalem and the Holy Places as its Court, is obvious. It involved, further, an immediate and sanguinary clash with the Roman garrisons throughout the land. It meant a vast uprising of the people, and the certainty of a punitive expedition, led by a Roman leader of resource, such as that which forty years later laid the city in ruins.

All these things belong to the broad outlines of a situation which was as inevitable as that night follows day. These facts could not have escaped the penetrating eyes of those responsible for the maintenance of the hard-won Jewish privileges under the Roman occupation. Caiaphas, as the acting High Priest, made an exceedingly acute observation in political statecraft when he said:

'It is expedient for you that one man should die for the people, and that the whole nation perish not' (John xi. 50).

But the personal consequences to Caiaphas and his family were hardly less distasteful. We do not know what changes in the Constitution of the Great Sanhedrin would have taken place under a truly Messianic régime. They would probably have been very considerable. But one thing is certain: the supreme ascendancy of the High Priest, as the arbiter of the national fortunes, would have suffered eclipse. Whatever aspects of its ancient and historic form the Hebrew Constitution might have retained, the real Dynast would have been the Messiah. As the national Deliverer and the supreme Representative of the God of Israel, His right to impose policy and to direct events would have been final and absolute. The prospect of the Nazarene Carpenter stepping into this unique and unparalleled seat of national power must have been profoundly disturbing to certain men (and women) who had an unquestioned interest in the maintenance of the *status quo*.

The problem, therefore, was to bring a conclusive case which was not only proof against possible criticism by the Seventy-one, but which also gave indisputable grounds for action under the Roman law.

In the search for this formula many witnesses were apparently examined and their testimony rejected as insufficient. Then came two witnesses with what seemed to be a particularly promising case. It involved two offences, each punishable by death under the Hebrew Code. Yet here again the same fatal weakness disclosed itself. It might pass the Sanhedrin, but would it pass the Roman Procurator? Most assuredly it would not. Something more serious than this apparently idle threat to destroy and rebuild the Temple would be necessary to secure the assent of Pilate to a penalty which had been expressly removed by Cæsar from sectarian hands.

The whole prosecution was thus obviously on the point of breaking down when the alert brain of Caiaphas conceived an expedient for saving the situation. It was illegal; but it was the last desperate throw of a man pushed to the very edge of endurance by the miscarriage of his plans. He applied the Oath of the Testimony, to which even silence itself was an unforgivable offence. It succeeded probably beyond his dreams, because in that fearless reply, 'I am', there flashed out the long-sought base of the deadliest of all charges before the Roman Procurator.

Cæsar might be indifferent to the somewhat eccentric utterances of an itinerant preacher. He could not be indifferent to a claimant for a throne. In the hush of the Court as the solemn words of the affirmation fell from the Prisoner's lips, certain other words were probably already forming in the mind of Caiaphas: 'If thou lettest this man go, thou art not Cæsar's friend.'

Chapter III

WHAT HAPPENED BEFORE
MIDNIGHT ON THURSDAY

I suggested on an earlier page that considerations of *time* played a peculiar and decisive part in determining the events which immediately preceded the death of Christ. If we wish to get at the real truth about this matter we must study it with our eyes, as it were, constantly upon the clock. Particularly is this the case when we approach two very important elements in the case: The dealings that the Jewish leaders had with *Judas* and later, with *Pontius Pilate*.

Both these men played a strange and, at first sight, an inexplicable role in the happenings of those twelve hours which closed the earthly life of Christ. Let us begin by considering the case of Judas.

The first thing which challenges thought about the affair of Judas is the very curious fact that Caiaphas and his friends should have found it necessary to employ him at all. Why does this man Judas come suddenly into the story? What was it that he could offer the Priests which was not theirs already by virtue of their official status? Why should even the trivial amount of the blood-money have been expended in securing his services?

These questions are vital, and affect profoundly our reading of the whole case. To regard Judas merely as a common informer, ready (for a consideration) to lead the authorities to the secret hiding-place of his erstwhile Friend and Leader, is absurd. Jesus was not in hiding. From the moment that He arrived, late on Friday afternoon, at Bethany no attempt seems to have been made to conceal His movements. He appears to have attended a dinner in His honour at the house of Simon the Leper, either on Saturday or Tuesday evening. On three successive days (Sunday, Monday, and Tuesday) He journeyed openly to Jerusalem, returning to Bethany each evening.

It is ridiculous to suppose, when even so early as Sunday morning vast numbers of the populace knew sufficient of His movements to throng the roadside to Jerusalem, that the leaders themselves were ignorant of His whereabouts. The fact obviously is that they knew very well. On any one of the four critical evenings they could have sent swiftly and secretly to Bethany and effected His arrest. Why was it not done? What was it for which they were waiting, and which only Judas could supply?

It is customary to meet these questions by laying stress upon that part of the answer which is recorded in the Gospels: the fear of the people. It does not appear, however, to have been widely discerned that, quite inevitably, this can only have been half of the real truth and that the other half has been withheld.

It must not be forgotten that the Gospels were written from material gathered mainly from the party identified with Christ. Judas died without disclosing his secret, and the Jewish leaders would hardly have been likely to betray it. But to suggest that all Judas did was to take the officers of the Sanhedrin to a lonely and secluded spot where they could secretly arrest Jesus, when they could have done it on their own initiative in the early hours of any morning at Bethany when the villagers were asleep, or at a suitable spot on the road across Olivet on any evening except Wednesday, or throughout Wednesday in the quiet groves of that tiny and peaceful hamlet, is to miss entirely the subtlety of the psychological factors which are here engaged.

To avoid any possibility of misunderstanding upon a vital point, let me say here that I would be the very last to deny that fear of the people carried great weight with the Jewish leaders. No one knew; no one could know what would be the political consequences of the forcible seizure of the person of One whom a large section of the populace regarded as the Messiah of prophecy. The whole situation was unprecedented, and one of extreme sensitiveness and

31

delicacy. Everything which these men did was done, as it were, with a furtive glance over the shoulder towards that unfathomable entity, the popular will.

But mere fear of the people does not explain some of the strangest things about the affair. Something which Judas told the Priests caused them to precipitate events at the last moment; to go through with the thing at a time which presented the maximum legal and official difficulties. It caused them to keep the strangest appointment between a 'wanted' man and His persecutors of which history gives us any cognizance. It led them to send to Him, an undefended man in a lonely and deserted garden at midnight, an imposing and even ridiculous display of force, supplemented by precautions, the meaning of which no one can mistake.

What does all this signify? Personally, I am convinced that beneath the ostensible and acknowledged fear of the people, there was a deeper and more potent fear—a fear which explains all their singular hesitancies and vacillations, until a welcome message reached their astonished ears—*the fear of Christ Himself*.

Lest this should seem to be a strange and unfamiliar thought, let us look at the facts. It is impossible to dissociate these men from the mental limitations and superstitions of their age. Whether the reader believes that the 'miracles' of Christ were actually performed or are merely the legendary ascriptions of a superstitious and unscientific age, the fact remains that the personal ascendancy and repute of Jesus during His own lifetime was immense. The stories of His cures of the blind, the paralytic and the possessed were widespread. They came from all parts of the country and were apparently implicitly accepted even in high quarters in Jerusalem. The fact that He possessed certain definite powers beyond the normal does not seem to have been doubted by His contemporaries.

It is difficult to read the Gospels impartially, particularly the closing chapters, without realizing that the nimbus of mystery which encircled the person of Jesus reacted most powerfully upon the plans of the leaders. They were dealing with an unknown and incalculable quantity, and their acts plainly show it. Throughout the four critical days which preceded the day of the arrest, when, had He wished, Jesus could have raised the city to an unimaginable pitch of tumult and excitement, they behaved as men under the compulsion of some secret fear. There is none of that swift and decisive grappling with a dangerous situation which we might have expected from men occupying the seat of power. Hesitancy and vacillation are written upon their acts. Even after the terrific and scathing denunciation on Tuesday afternoon, they left the initiative with Christ. Indeed, it is one of the master facts of this strange narrative that the initiative remained with Christ even to the end.

Personally, I cannot avoid feeling that, in all their dealings with Jesus, these men were apprehensive of something happening which they did not care to define. They seem to have been in some doubt whether even a considerable force would be adequate to take Him, and that in the last resort He might even prove to be unarrestable. This impression is unmistakably strengthened by their singular behaviour in the matter of Judas.

Nothing can be clearer than that, throughout the week which preceded the arrest, there was some impediment which led to the event being postponed to the eleventh hour, when in the nature of things their difficulties were increased. The first interview with Judas seems to have promised well because we are told (Mark xiv. 11):

'And they, when they heard it, were glad, and promised to give him money. And he sought how he might conveniently deliver him unto them.'

If we are to follow the chronology of the Gospels this happened at the very latest on Tuesday, after the dinner at the house of Simon the Leper. Yet still no overt move was made. It was not until late on Thursday night, when Judas hurried from the Supper Room, that their hesitation changed into resolution, and a phase of intense and feverish activity set in.

Now it is just here that the element of time becomes so

important and illuminating. If the arrest of Jesus had followed within a short time of His arrival in the Garden, it would be a legitimate assumption that Judas's part of the pact was limited to warning the authorities where He could be found late on Thursday evening and to accompanying the arrest party for purposes of identification. This assumption presupposes that it was a deliberate part of the leaders' plans to effect the arrest on the last evening before the Feast, so as to give the minimum opportunity for a popular reaction.

Plausible as this explanation appears at first sight, it will not stand examination. The facts point in quite a different direction. Suppose that the understanding which the priests had with Judas was this:

'We intend to take Him on Thursday night. Remain with Him until you are absolutely sure of His movements, and then come quickly and tell us. We will do the rest.'

It is obvious that a plot of this kind implies that all needful preparations for so important an event would have been made. The officers of the Temple Guard detailed to accompany the expedition would have been warned and have been in readiness. Within a few minutes of the receipt of the message the arrest party would have been mobilized and ready to move off.

Did things take this course? Most assuredly they did not. An extraordinary and intensely suggestive *delay of several hours* intervened between the time when Judas withdrew from the supper party, and the arrival of a motley and miscellaneous contingent (armed, one might say, to the teeth) in the Garden of Gethsemane. What is the historical explanation of that delay? Consider the situation carefully and mark its strangeness, for it is full of strange, and otherwise unaccountable things.

First, and foremost, there is the delay of something approaching three hours between the departure of Judas from the supper chamber and the arrival of the arrest party in Gethsemane. That this period could hardly have been shorter will be apparent if we piece together the unmistakably historical events which intervened. I have already referred (page 14) to the length of time which must have elapsed in the Garden itself to allow for the thrice-repeated waking of the disciples. The fact that these men went to sleep at all points to a very late hour and a long vigil before fatigue overcame the natural desire to keep awake and to share with their Master whatever danger or experiences the night might bring. We do not know how long they resisted the temptation, but when sleep would no longer be denied, we can hardly assume that less than half an hour elapsed between each waking. This, with the half-hour roughly occupied in the walk from the city, brings us to two hours. To this we must add the time required by the conversations in the Supper Room after Judas had left and (if St. John's account is trustworthy) by the lovely nocturnal prayer in the street without, before the party finally wended its way to the gate of the city.

If anyone will sit down in the twilight of some quiet evening and read through this section of the narrative, and reflect upon it as he goes, he will find it all amazingly true to life. But he will find also that the set pace of the thing cannot be rushed or hurried. He will be constantly tempted by stray words and allusions rather to slow down the pace and to allow a longer period than we are now contemplating. Can we imagine, for example, the disciples on arriving at Gethsemane upon some obviously strange and mysterious errand, lying down and going to sleep forthwith? Human beings are not built that way. There would be a period during which whispered questions and vague surmises would pass from lip to lip. There would be long moments of anxious waiting and wondering, until one by one, from sheer fatigue, they dropped to sleep.

Now this very significant gap of at least three hours in the movement of an otherwise tense and closely-knit drama has to be explained. It is imperative that we should know what Judas was doing all the time, and especially *why, when the expedition did at last set out, Judas knew where he would find Jesus.* In some ways this is the master fact of the situation. When we know that we have the key to what is surely the strangest episode in history.

Primarily, the impression which the records give is that the message which Judas brought found the Jewish leaders in some way unprepared. Personally, I cannot escape that impression, and further reflection only serves to deepen it. Had it been a deliberate part of the Jewish plan to postpone the arrest of Jesus until the latest moment on Thursday and to carry it through regardless of consequences, there would have been signs of preparedness and organization. These men did not know where they might not have to send to secure their Prisoner. They might even have to go as far as Bethany. Indeed, the probabilities were strongly in favour of that course, for who could have foreseen that the 'wanted' man would wait conveniently in a neighbouring garden? In this case Nemesis would have swiftly overtaken Jesus when the secret rendezvous was known, as it must have been within a few minutes of Judas's departure from the supper-table.

Instead of this we get a delay running into hours, a circumstance which might easily have been fatal to the success of the whole expedition. Had the wanted man been any ordinary fugitive it would have failed.

The more closely the facts of this momentous episode are considered, the stronger the impression becomes that the visit of Judas to the Priests that night, while not wholly unexpected, put their problem in a new and urgent light. Time was needed for consultation, for the taking of great decisions, for the improvisation of means, and when the expedition to Gethsemane did at last move off, it did so at the earliest possible moment consistent with these hurried preparations. I submit that the narratives, as preserved in the four Gospels, bear that interpretation and no other.

Now there are two factors in this very interesting situation which are unmistakably historical, and which, dovetailing as they do into each other, explain the delay. The first is that the message which Judas brought from the supper room contained a new and surprising piece of information which completely resolved the hesitation and doubts of the rulers. The second is that Christ Himself was challenging and indeed facilitating His own arrest.

Whatever may have been the actual words employed, the burden of the conversation which Judas had with the priests must have been this:

'He is thinking and talking of death. He is going to the garden at the foot of Olivet and will wait there till I come. Make your arrangements quickly and I will take you to Him.'

There seems to be no escaping this inference because it is buttressed at both ends by the silent but unimpeachable witness of the behaviour of the two principal actors in the drama. We have documentary track of both parties. We *know* that Judas took the expedition unerringly to the groves of Gethsemane, despite the darkness and the extreme lateness of the hour. We *know* that Jesus waited in those very groves, to the exhaustion of His friends, and would apparently have gone on waiting even to the dawn.

We do not ordinarily get a situation like that without implying something which, from sheer poverty of language, I must call an understanding. Let no one hastily jump to the conclusion that there was a kind of pact between Jesus and His betrayer. I do not think that it was like that in the least. Jesus was a master of psychology, and His irrevocable determination to deliver Himself to His accusers that night was accomplished by infinitely subtler means. But when Judas left the Upper Room on an ostensibly innocent mission[1] he knew of a surety two things. He knew that Jesus was going to the Garden of Gethsemane, and he knew also that His spirit was already bending to the Cross. These two great facts coming in fortuitous combination were his great opportunity and his supreme temptation.

His alert brain was quick to perceive that this was better

[1] It adds greatly to the verisimilitude of the story when we remember that the arrangement to meet in Gethsemane was probably arrived at quite naturally and in the ordinary course of events. Judas had apparently certain duties to perform on behalf of the band which necessitated his absence for a while, and it is natural that a place should be appointed where they should meet prior to returning in a body across the hills to Bethany. The Garden of Gethsemane was a peculiarly appropriate place for the rendezvous, because it stood in the triangle between the two most frequented routes over the shoulder of Olivet to the little hamlet. Both of these mountain tracks, in addition to the main road (which skirted the garden), led to Bethany.

news than he had ever hoped to carry to his new masters. The impediment was gone. For this night at least Jesus would not resist arrest. The mood of surrender was upon Him. It only remained to send quickly to achieve their purpose.

With this new fact uppermost in his mind, Judas, in all human probability, hurried direct to the High Priest's house. His private business, even if he now intended to go through with it, could wait. It was of supreme importance that the machinery of state should be put into action without delay.

What, then, would be the effect of this intelligence upon Caiaphas and the little coterie of Sadducees whose interests were so closely involved in the death of Christ? Fortunately we are able to define the answer to this question pretty accurately, because there were two fundamental things about the situation which, from their standpoint, out-weighed every other consideration, and governed their policy.

In the first place it would have been fatal to their interests to have made an *unsuccessful* attempt to arrest Jesus at this particular juncture. By this I mean that, if, after launching their bolt, it had failed through causes which could even remotely be attributed to the supernatural, the damage to their prestige would have been irreparable.

Secondly, it would have been even more dangerous to have arrested Christ, and have been compelled to hold Him without trial during the seven days prescribed by the Feast. This they simply dared not do. Jerusalem at Feast times, with its huge non-resident population, was notoriously turbulent and prone to high feelings. They could probably count upon the popular stupefaction occasioned by so re-sounding an event as the arrest of Jesus lasting a few hours, but reaction would follow swiftly.

To men confronted with these alternatives, the news which Judas Iscariot brought late on Thursday night both ameliorated their problem and increased its practical difficulties tenfold. It ameliorated it because it gave them the assurance and certainty of arrest. It told them that the time of their opportunity had come. It increased their difficulties because it came at such a late hour as to render it almost certain that they must face the second and more deadly of their perils.

The practical question which arose immediately, therefore, was probably this: 'Can we possibly carry the thing through all its inevitable legal stages in time to secure execution before sundown to-morrow?' It was a very big and complicated issue, not lightly to be answered.

I cannot see that this question could have been answered off-hand even by the High Priest himself, fortified as he undoubtedly was by the secular wisdom and long experience of his father-in-law Annas. The thing demanded consultation at least with the representative men of the different groups constituting the Sanhedrin. The situation was so entirely without precedent. And failure to carry the whole process through, even by a hair's breadth, involved consequences of a very dangerous order.

Whatever else, therefore, had to be done, some considerable part of those three hours must have been occupied in hurried consultations, in swift passings to and fro between the executive sitting at the High Priest's house, and those indispensable leaders of Jewish thought upon whom they must rely for ratification in the Sanhedrin. All this is written plainly between the lines of the narrative. But was there something else? Personally, I think there was.

Whatever interpretation we put upon the circumstances leading up to the arrest of Christ it seems to me certain that, before the fateful word was given to the arrest party to proceed to Gethsemane, *some communication must have taken place between the Jewish leaders and Pontius Pilate*.

It is against everything which we know about the character of Pilate and the nature of the Roman occupation to assume that a serious case like this could have been thrust upon Pilate early on Friday morning without his knowledge and without first ascertaining his readiness to take it.

The fact that none of the four Gospel writers refers to a prior consultation with Pilate is not difficult to understand. They were writing from their own particular standpoint.

The assent of Pilate to the Jewish plans would seem to them of small moment, and was in any case an administrative detail in which they had probably little interest. But the moment we put ourselves in the place of the priests we see how very vital it was that, late as the hour might be, the consent and co-operation of the Procurator should be obtained.

If anyone feels that the received narrative does not quite carry this conviction, let me enjoin him to consider carefully one small but very significant circumstance. There is a deeply rooted tradition in the early Christian literature (supported, of course, by St. John's very detailed account of the Roman trial) that Pilate departed from the usual practice upon this occasion by coming out to the Jews, so as to meet their ceremonial objection to entering the Court of the Stranger on that day. The reason was of course that time did not permit of the necessary purification prior to the Feast. If this be an historical detail it can only mean one thing, viz. that had it not been for the supreme and urgent case of Christ, Pilate would have held no Court upon that day. It would have been absurd, in the ordinary course of events, to hold judicial proceedings on a day when, in the nature of the case, the principal officers and witnesses could not be present. The fact that Pilate did sit on that day, and that without apparent demur he proceeded to hear the case in the open space outside the Prætorium, points to an understanding of a very definite kind.

Thus, if we try to get into the inner mind of the priests and look at the very complicated problem which they had to solve at short notice, we shall see that some kind of communication with Pilate was inevitable. They were suddenly offered the opportunity of arresting Jesus under unexpectedly favourable conditions. It was night, and the populace were preoccupied with the preparations for the Feast. Moreover, the prospective Prisoner Himself was strangely willing, and in some inexplicable way seemed to be facilitating their plans. From the purely political side the course was clear. The door which they expected they would have to force stood open.

On the other hand, the legal difficulties were immense. The problem of assembling the Court after nightfall, of getting together the necessary witnesses, and of arranging for a full session of the Sanhedrin the next morning, called for hard thinking and rapid organization. Much would necessarily have to be left to chance, and to the hope of things working out roughly to plan. But the broad lines of their programme would have to be settled before releasing the bolt which was to put their fortunes to the test.

But even when the bare minimum of their essentials had been settled—the arrest, the midnight hearing to formulate the charge and secure conviction, the early meeting of the Sanhedrin to ratify the finding—there still remained one supreme question to which a definite answer must be forthcoming. Could they secure the Roman conviction in time to guarantee crucifixion before the Feast? Would Pilate be willing to hear the case under the peculiar conditions which they were bound to impose? Would he insist on a full trial or could they count upon a formal endorsement of a finding previously arrived at by their own Courts?

Such questions as these would ordinarily be settled through official channels and as a matter of administrative routine. There must have been some kind of calendar for the trial of Jewish prisoners, whose cases necessitated review by the Procurator, and in the preparation of this calendar Pilate's personal convenience would invariably be consulted.

The extreme urgency of the present case, however, precluded reliance upon these channels. It was already very late in the evening. If the conviction was to go through, it was imperative that some kind of provisional arrangement should be come to with the Procurator to hear the case early the next morning.

There was probably only one man in Jerusalem who could seek an audience with Pilate at an hour ordinarily devoted to his private pleasure. That man was Caiaphas, the High Priest, and it was Caiaphas, in all human probability, who went. He alone could present with the full authority of his

41

supreme office the high reasons of state behind the prosecution.

It may seem a small matter whether the titular chief of the Jewish nation visited Pilate at a very late hour on that memorable evening or not. But if things took the course which we shall discuss in the next chapter, it will be found that that unrecorded visit has profound and far-reaching significance. It explains something which on any other supposition is wholly inexplicable. I mean the very curious behaviour of Pilate next day during the critical hours which decided the fate of Christ.

Chapter IV

A PSYCHOLOGICAL PARALLELOGRAM
OF FORCES

If anyone thinks that in approaching the trial of Jesus of
Nazareth by Pontius Pilate he is approaching the simple
and the obvious he is making a big miscalculation.

This thing is very subtle. Outwardly it has all the placidity
of still waters, but beneath the apparent stillness there are
deep and hidden currents which make it incomparably the
greatest and most profoundly interesting psychological
study in history. We do not get rid of the mystery of Christ
when we bring Him to the Roman bar; we increase it tenfold.

The first hint that there is something curious about this
story which is not directly disclosed by the narratives comes,
strangely enough, not from the behaviour of the Jews, or
even of the Prisoner Himself, but from the behaviour of
Pilate. I remember reading through the four accounts side
by side, not once but many times, trying to discover what it
was that subconsciously stamped the story of this trial as
peculiar. And every time I read them the conviction grew
that the hidden and disturbing element lay in what, for
want of a better phrase, I must call the unsatisfactory alignment of Pilate's behaviour, as uniformly reported in the
Gospels, with his known character and antecedents.

We know something at least about the previous history of
this brusque and uncultured soldier of the Roman Empire.
A tradition, which may not be very reliable, says that he was
born at Seville in Spain. He came of a fighting family, was a
member of the *ordo equester* and served for a time under
Germanicus in Germany. During a prolonged stay in Rome
he seems to have captured the affection of a Roman girl of

very high connections, Claudia Procula, whom he was destined to marry, and of whom we shall hear more shortly. As the illegitimate daughter of Claudia, the third wife of Tiberius, Claudia Procula was the grand-daughter of Augustus Cæsar. It is obvious from the sequel that this accidental connection with the ruling house served Pilate's personal interests in an unexpected degree, for in A.D. 26, on the recommendation of Sejanus, he was appointed Procurator of Judea, and in accepting the post he applied for and obtained the very unusual privilege of taking his wife with him.

Such are the few but suggestive facts which we know about Pilate prior to his coming to Judea. When, however, we reach the ten critical years of his life with which history is chiefly concerned, we begin to get light thrown upon him from new directions. Three episodes stand out during that stormy decade. There was the affair of the Roman Ensigns; there was the affair of the 'Corban'; and there was the affair of the votive shields. To these may be added the incident of the Samaritan imposture which occasioned his recall and ultimate banishment. Each of these episodes in its way illustrates and defines the man with whom we have to deal.

If anyone will read carefully and impartially the contemporary classical accounts of these events, paying particular heed to the *behaviour* of Pilate, as distinct from the motives ascribed to him, he will form a very definite impression of a somewhat coarse, rather tactless and very obstinate man, a man to whom authority denoted power to enforce his own will rather than responsibility and consideration towards others. There is not a trace of that tact in handling foreign and subject peoples which characterized Julius Cæsar and certain other far-seeing high-born Romans. He was the embodiment of that personal aggressiveness with which men and women, thrust into a position of authority which exceeds their powers, so often seek to attain their ends.

His obstinacy and complete lack of ordinary political insight come out very strikingly in the matter of the Roman ensigns. We do not know what prompted him to send the ensigns and other insignia of the Legions into Jerusalem.

But the fact that he did so at night suggests that he knew that there was going to be trouble. When the trouble came and he was practically besieged at Cæsarea for six days and six nights, he made apparently not the slightest effort to arrive at a solution by discussion or argument. His only reply on the sixth day was to surround the deputation by armed force. When he found as a result of this belated test that he could only get his way by wholesale massacre (so fanatical was the objection to graven images in Jerusalem) he capitulated and the ensigns were withdrawn.

It is fortunate that we are able to compare the behaviour of Pilate in this matter with the handling of an almost identical situation by another Roman soldier, Petronius. The story is told with some fullness by Josephus. The salient feature about this narrative is the manifest recognition by Petronius that there were deep-seated moral forces behind the native Jewish demonstration with which even the political might and statecraft of Rome must reckon. He tried to remove the obstacles by fair reasoning and private conference. He had an infinitely stronger incentive than Pilate to enforce his will, for he had been definitely commissioned by a mad Emperor to place the Imperial image in the Jewish Temple, and failure to do so invited unpleasant consequences. When he ran against the same unshakeable rock which confronted Pilate he wrote a report to Caius which not only stamps him as a very brave man, but unquestionably raised the prestige of Rome in the East.

But the point that I want to bring out is that the difference between Petronius' handling of this delicate affair and Pilate's action in closely similar circumstances is characteristic and deeply instructive. It marks the whole difference between two types of mind which were poles asunder. All Pilate's affairs were handled with the same lack of mental resilience and understanding.

Take, for example, the affair of the 'Corban,' or sacred treasury. The object for which Pilate took this money was in itself a commendable one—the financing of an aqueduct from the Pools of Solomon to the interior of the City. The Jews were as much interested in a sure and safe water supply for Jerusalem as anybody. The problem had occupied successive kings and statesmen for centuries, and more than one exclusively Jewish attempt had been made to solve it.

The question of finding the money for this very necessary public work would not have been difficult if put squarely to the authorities. But Pilate must needs raid the 'Corban', a fund devoted exclusively to religious purposes. When the populace quite naturally revolted he provoked a needlessly sanguinary and fatal tumult by sending soldiers disguised as civilians into the mob.

We get precisely the same characteristic and implacable cast of mind in the matter of the votive shields which Pilate installed in the Herodian Palace. There was apparently not the slightest attempt to understand or appreciate the deepseated character of the religious objection to these tablets, or any desire even to discuss it. It was only when a letter from the chief men of the nation to Tiberius brought a strong reproof from the Emperor that Pilate gave way.

There is a hint, too, in the Gospels of an affair in which Pilate mingled the blood of certain Galileans with their 'sacrifices'. We do not know to what this refers, but it agrees pretty closely with what we know of his temperament, and bears a resemblance to his handling of the Samaritan affair as recorded by Philo.

Such, then, are the lineaments of Pontius Pilate as they emerge from the only independent and secular accounts we have of him. They are all amazingly self-consistent and true to type.

Now directly we turn to the Gospel accounts of the trial of Jesus by this man we get an immediate and unmistakable impression that the personality revealed does not lie four square upon the impression which we have previously formed of him. Somehow this does not seem to be the real Pilate—haughty, overbearing, truculent—who is trying the Man of Death. He seems so remarkably anxious to conciliate the Jews, and yet so unaccountably reluctant to concede their wishes. He gives the impression of a man being tugged between two opposite and irreconcilable forces.

Personally, I cannot escape the feeling that Pilate did not want to touch this thing. He had one idea paramount in his mind—*to get Christ acquitted*, somehow, and at all costs. We see this motif running through everything—the attempt to shift the matter to Herod, the thrice-acclaimed innocence of the Prisoner, the washing of hands—the last desperate attempt to substitute Barabbas, as a sop to the insistence and clamour of the people. It was only when the sinister cry, 'Thou art not Cæsar's friend', began to make itself heard above the tumult that a new and greater fear triumphed over the one that had been gnawing at his mind.

What is the explanation of this apparently inconsistent behaviour of a man who normally had a very strong will of his own and who did not readily brook opposition to it? Why does Pilate, the tyrant of secular history, appear as Pilate the irresolute in the pages of the Gospels?

I do not think that we shall ever reach the true explanation of this phenomenon until we take into account various personal matters on the side of Pilate, and especially what probably took place in his own household on the evening before the trial.

It will be remembered that in tracing the causes of certain peculiar and otherwise inexplicable delays connected with the arrest of Jesus, we reached the conclusion that Pilate must have been warned of what was about to take place, and that the interview at which this was done could not have occurred much earlier than eleven o'clock in the evening.

Strong as the evidence for this unreported interview with Pilate undoubtedly is, it is strengthened by one small but highly significant circumstance—the fact that Claudia Procula was in the Herodian Palace that night. It is an extraordinarily suggestive thing that the only reference to Claudia in this particular connection which has survived the centuries should have told us that *she dreamed about Jesus Christ on the night before His death*.

So long as we think of the Roman trial of Jesus as developing along the traditional lines (so often inferred from the Gospels), by which the Jews without prior arrangement brought Christ on Friday morning to the bar of Pilate, the reference to Procula seems utterly illogical and its substance improbable. But directly we put these events in their natural sequence the truth seems to look us in the face. For consider the most likely trend of events upon that memorable night.

Pilate was 'in town', not for a brief flying visit, but for the full ten days ordinarily covered by the Feast. The probability, therefore, that Caludia came with him is very strong, even if we had not St. Matthew's definite statement that such was the case. Their friends in the foreign capital were undoubtedly few. A man occupying Pilate's position had to restrict severely the circle of his intimate acquaintances, and the two were necessarily thrown much upon each other's company.

We shall probably not be very far wrong if on this particular night we imagine them sitting before the fire in one of the spacious apartments of their private suite in the Palace, for we know from Peter's warming of his hands that the evening was chilly. To appreciate fully what then happened we must remember the peculiar limitations of time which the problem imposes. We know from the Gospel records that Pilate heard the case very early on Friday morning. The hurried visit of Judas to the High Priest's house took place probably between eight and nine o'clock, for the supper party lingered on after he had gone, and we have still the two hours' waiting in the Garden to account for. If the decision to arrest Jesus was taken as the result of the information which Judas carried to the Priests (and we have the strongest reasons for believing such to be the case) it is clear that Pilate must have been approached some time between nine o'clock and, say, eleven-thirty. How else could arrangements involving the personal movements of the Procurator early the following morning have been consummated?

As I have suggested in a previous chapter, there was probably only one person in Jerusalem who could safely intrude himself upon the privacy of Pilate's household at such a late hour, and then only upon urgent political grounds. That man was the High Priest himself. Indeed, I do not see how Pilate's services in this matter could have

been secured at all at such extremely short notice, apart
from urgent personal representations from the highest
authority in the Jewish State.

It would seem, therefore, that we shall be well within the
margin of historic probability if we assume that some time
between the hours of nine o'clock and eleven, and probably
much nearer the latter than the former, a distinguished
caller presented himself at the Herodian Palace. Possibly
the visitor was shown direct into the private apartment, but
more probably Pilate went out to an ante-chamber to meet
him.

Then, as I conceive it, in a few anxious minutes for the
powers in Jerusalem, the outline of the impending *démarche*
was disclosed. An important political offender was to be
arrested that night. The trial would be consummated the
next morning, and a verdict involving the extreme penalty
was probable. Would Pilate consent to review the case at an
early hour so that the necessary ratification might be given
in time to secure death by sunset?

Probably also some conversation took place on the
difficult question of defilement. It was not permissible for
those charged with high duties in the Temple to enter the
court of the stranger on this particular day. Yet the matter
was urgent. The alternative to summary jurisdiction (having
regard to the character of the City's huge temporary population) was an insurrection. Would Pilate be prepared on
this occasion to come out to the deputation who would
present the Prisoner and the finding of the Jewish Court?

With the discussion of such questions as these from
twenty minutes to half an hour probably went by, and with
the departure of his visitor Pilate returned to the fireside.
Now does anyone with personal knowledge of the imme-
morial characteristics of women suppose for a moment that
an incident like this would pass without Claudia wanting to
know something about it? She would not have been a
woman if she had not been curious, and we may be practically certain that before they retired to rest that night some
conversation took place upon the unexpected visit, the
identity of the prisoner, and the reasons (satisfactory or

otherwise) behind the arrest. Anything that foreboded trouble between her husband and the Jews had a special interest for Procula.

When, therefore, Claudia retired to her room in the late evening, it would be, almost certainly, with the thought of Jesus in her mind. And when she awoke next morning after a vivid and painful dream, to find that Pilate had already risen and left the Palace, she knew where he had gone and the delicate matter in which he was engaged. It was at this moment that, according to St. Matthew, she sent him a message—almost telegraphic in its brevity and urgency— designed to convey in the fewest possible words her own grave apprehensions and the course which she thought he ought to take:

'Have thou nothing to do with that righteous man: for I have suffered many things this day in a dream because of him.'

So far we have a logical and intelligible sequence of events. Is the sequel equally logical? I submit that it is. For the characteristic which immediately strikes us about Claudia's message to Pilate, as reported by St. Matthew, is its *urgency*. The words are those of someone who is manifestly writing in great haste, and who wants to convey in the fewest possible words a message at once grave and immediate. Indeed, it would be difficult to imagine a sentence of greater brevity which would have conveyed so precisely the information which Procula apparently desired to get through to Pilate. She wanted to warn him primarily and above all else *not to touch this thing*. She seems to have been under something more than an impression that Pilate was going to commit Christ to his enemies, and that at an early stage in the proceedings. Hence the need for her instant warning.

I will not waste time here arguing the obvious point that, if Claudia knew of the arrest overnight in the circumstances suggested above, that in itself is an adequate and sufficient cause for the dream. But I do want to draw attention to a very significant detail, viz. that the dream would not have had the instant terror for Procula, on awakening early the next morning, if she had not known, or had exceptionally strong reasons for suspecting, that Pilate was going to hand over the Prisoner to His enemies.

The whole tenor of the message suggests this:

'Have thou *nothing to do* with that *righteous* man, for I have suffered many things this day in a dream because of him.'

However we construe the words, they could only have been written by a woman who was anxious to avert something which she was afraid was going to happen. The facts seem to point to one conclusion, viz. that Claudia had reason to believe that Pilate intended to ratify the finding of the Jewish Tribunal without rehearing, or at any rate with a bare minimum of official formality. In other words, that he had practically decided to confirm the Jewish decision, and had probably already given assurances to that effect overnight.

I confess that my own mind was prepared somewhat for this conclusion by the very nature of the peculiar political situation which drove the Priests to take the extreme measure which they did. I cannot help feeling that the principal thing which Caiaphas wanted to know before he sanctioned the arrest was whether Pilate would do this very thing. If on this particular occasion, and upon the personal representation of the High Priest that the offence committed was worthy of death, Pilate would consent to ratify the finding of the Sanhedrin, the whole thing could be settled and done with before sunset. If not, then no one could tell what delays might take place, and it would be safer to postpone the arrest to a more convenient season. The fact that the arrest did take place according to plan seems to point to the Jews having received assurance upon this point.

But what I was not prepared for—what, indeed, came to me personally as a surprise—was the discovery that the narratives of the Roman trial itself unmistakably bear out and confirm this view.

The matter is one which will repay very careful study.

If anyone will take the four Gospel records of the trial of Jesus by Pontius Pilate, and after putting them side by side, make a careful comparative study of them, he will find them absolutely unanimous upon one point, viz. that Pilate addressed to Jesus the question: 'Art thou the King of the Jews?'

Now this is significant because the two earlier evangelists give no hint that Pilate had ever been told what the charge was. Both St. Matthew and St. Mark, with their accustomed brevity and that complete absence of subsidiary detail which is characteristic of them, described Pilate as asking this leading question at once thus:

St. Mark	*St. Matthew*
'And straightway in the morning the chief priests with the elders and scribes, and the whole council, held a consultation, and bound Jesus, and carried him away, and delivered him up to Pilate. And Pilate asked him, Art thou the King of the Jews?'	'Now when morning was come, all the chief priests and the elders of the people took counsel against Jesus to put him to death: and they bound him, and led him away, and delivered him up to Pilate the governor. . . . Now Jesus stood before the governor: and the governor asked him saying, Art thou the King of the Jews?'

It is perfectly obvious that this could not, in any circumstances have been the *beginning* of these proceedings. Both of these Synoptic writers have jumped over something which it is exceedingly important for us to know, viz. how this vital and rather peculiar question was led up to, and what it was that caused Pilate to ask it.

Fortunately we have two other independent versions to which we can turn and I will ask the reader to examine these with some care. To facilitate comparison we will set them out fully below:

St. Luke

'And the whole company of them rose up, and brought him before Pilate. And they began to accuse him, saying, We found this man perverting our nation, and forbidding to give tribute to Cæsar, and saying that he himself is Christ a king. And Pilate asked him, saying, Art thou the King of the Jews?'

A Psychological Parallelogram of Forces

St. John

'Pilate therefore went out unto them, and saith, What accusation bring ye against this man? They answered and said unto him, If this man were not an evil-doer, we should not have delivered him up unto thee. Pilate therefore said unto them, Take him yourselves, and judge him according to your law. The Jews said unto him, It is not lawful for us to put any man to death: that the word of Jesus might be fulfilled, which he spake, signifying by what manner of death he should die. Pilate therefore entered again into the palace, and called Jesus, and said unto him, Art thou the King of the Jews?'

Two things stand out from these accounts. First, they offer a much fuller and more intelligible account of what happened. But secondly, and chiefly, Pilate's question comes, as we knew it must after some preliminary interchange of argument with the Jews. It is that preliminary phase of the trial to which I want to direct particular attention.

If we were left solely with the evidence and witness of St. Luke, we should have to assume that immediately the priests brought their Prisoner to the bar they launched their general accusation thus:

'We found this man perverting our nation, and forbidding to give tribute to Cæsar, and saying that he himself is Christ a king.'

Let it be said here that, psychologically, this would have been a perfectly natural and satisfactory opening to the case, and if no other data were available, we should be justified, nay, even compelled, to assume that it began in that way. But there is something in the version of the Fourth Gospel which arrests attention, because it throws new light on the way in which the case was presented from the Jewish side. It is not that the writer of John's version contradicts what the Synoptic writers have said. On the contrary, he confirms it. But he seems to begin a little further back, and he supplies a link in the narrative which is missing from the other three.

He states first what on every ground we must regard as most probable, viz. that when Jesus was brought to Pilate, the Prisoner Himself was conducted into the Palace while the Priests and other accusers remained outside.

After a short interval, according to St. John, Pilate came out and put the formal question to the Jews: 'What accusation do you bring against this man?' This was the definite opening of the Roman trial, for it was an essential part of the Roman system that a public *Accusatio* should be made, followed by the *Interrogatio* of the judge, and the *Excusatio* of the prisoner.

The reply of the Priests to this question is so significant and suggestive that I do not think that due weight has been given to it. The priests replied:

> '*If this man were not an evil-doer, we should not have delivered him up unto thee.*'

Before we consider what this phrase means, let us look again closely at the two narratives printed on pages 52–53. It is obvious even upon a cursory reading that there is a *gap* in St. John's version following the words *It is not lawful for us to put any man to death.* In no conceivable circumstance could Pilate have passed direct from this evasive and resentful answer to his leading question to Jesus: Art thou then a King? There must have been some intervening conversation to have led up to it.

Fortunately the missing sentence has been furnished by St. Luke, and we may therefore fill the gap as shown in the complete narrative printed below:

RECONSTRUCTED NARRATIVE OF THE OPENING OF THE
ROMAN TRIAL

Presentation of the Prisoner to Pilate:	'They lead Jesus therefore from Caiaphas into the palace: and it was early; and they themselves entered not into the palace, that they might not be defiled, but might eat the passover.'
Pilate's demand for the 'Accusatio':	'Pilate therefore went out unto them, and saith, What accusation bring ye against this man?'

A Psychological Parallelogram of Forces

The Priests' obvious reluctance to produce a charge:	'They answered and said unto him. If this man were not an evil-doer, we should not have delivered him up unto thee.'
Pilate's rejoinder:	'Pilate therefore said unto them, Take him yourselves, and judge him according to your law.'
The Priests' reply with an improvised charge:	'The Jews said unto him, It is not lawful for us to put any man to death.
	'And they began to accuse him, saying, We found this man perverting our nation, and forbidding to give tribute to Cæsar, and saying that he himself is Christ a king.'
Pilate's question to the Prisoner:	'Pilate therefore entered again into the palace, and called Jesus, and said unto him, Art thou the King of the Jews?'

Not only does this reconstructed narrative contain the essential facts recorded by the four writers in the order in which they give them, but it is really the *only* account which we possess of these proceedings, for, as an examination of the documents will show, the four writers are almost unanimous when their particular point of entry has been reached. Moreover, it reads like an authentic piece of history.

With this description now before us we can attempt a reconstruction of an incident which, both historically and psychologically, is probably without precedent in the annals of the world.

* * * * *

The first definite act of the drama of which we have historical record is the bringing of Jesus from the place of His confinement (probably the High Priest's House) to the place of trial. This occupied, perhaps, twenty minutes, but as it was still quite early probably few people witnessed the little procession as it made its way swiftly through the narrow streets of Old Jerusalem. The Procurator, himself astir early, was awaiting the deputation. On arrival at the

55

gate of the Palace we must probably allow for a halt of a few moments for the examination of credentials, after which the Prisoner was conducted alone, under a Roman escort, to the presence chamber of Pilate. Meanwhile, the deputation and their attendants waited without.

*   *   *   *   *

We come now to a point of considerable interest. After a brief interval, Pilate himself came out to the Jewish deputation and put the question: 'What accusation do you bring against this man?' As I have said above, this was an unmistakable indication that Pilate intended to re-hear the case, and it seems to have aroused intense resentment on the side of the Priests—for their answer is not only lacking in proper respect for Pilate, who was acting fully within his duty, but points to their having a special grievance against him in this matter.

'If this man were not an evil-doer, we should not have delivered him up unto thee.'

Assuming, as I do, the historicity of this reply, it seems to me that there is only one possible interpretation to be placed upon it. The Priests resented Pilate's sudden determination to re-hear the case. They were clearly under the impression that he would not insist on a formal restatement of the case against Jesus, and they appear to have come without any prepared or public accusation at all. If we were to attempt a broad but, I think, quite legitimate paraphrase, we may regard the priests as saying: 'Can't you be satisfied with the finding of our Court, that this man is an evil-doer? Why re-open the case when we ourselves have found him worthy of death?'

To this Pilate made a very subtle reply:

'Take him yourselves, and judge him according to your law.'

The inevitable answer to this skilful counterthrust was a renewed demand for ratification:

'It is not lawful for us to put any man to death.'

56

It would seem then that, realizing the hopelessness of getting what they wanted without the production of a case:

'They began to accuse him, saying, We found this man perverting our nation, and forbidding to give tribute to Cæsar, and saying that he himself is Christ a King.'

The mention of the words 'a King' at last gave Pilate something to work upon, and he retired into the Palace to put the historic question to Jesus: 'Art thou the King of the Jews?'

Now there are two things about this episode which call for special notice.

Firstly, it reads like a transcript from life.

Secondly, the manifest resentment and surprise shown by the Priests when Pilate indicated his intention of re-hearing the case, or at any rate of closely examining the Prisoner, points unmistakably to something resembling an understanding. They would hardly have made so insolent and pointed a reference to ratification of their own sentence if they had not been led in some way to expect it.

But when we place this fact in juxtaposition with that other fact—the urgency of Claudia's reported message to her husband—its intrinsic probability is increased. We begin to see why Claudia was so anxious to get her message into her husband's hands before it was too late. For if events took the course which it seems they must have done, Claudia knew not merely the identity of the Prisoner when she retired to rest, but she knew also that Pilate was contemplating (if he had not already promised) the ratification of the Jewish sentence. It was this that gave the whole point to her hurried communication. She wanted to tell him at all costs not to take that course.

If this be a true reading of this remarkable episode, then one thing stands out clearly. The message which Claudia Procula sent to Pontius Pilate on the morning of the Crucifixion changed in certain essential respects the course of history. If Pilate actually received this message he must have done so shortly after his arrival at the place of trial, for highly strung women are generally light sleepers, and

the whole tenor of the message suggests its hurried indite-
ment on waking. That Pilate had come down to the audience
chamber intending formally to ratify the Jewish sentence
seems to me certain. Before the deputation arrived, however,
something happened which caused him to change his mind.
But not only so. Psychological states have the peculiarity
when suddenly challenged of swinging to their opposite
extremes, and Pilate throughout his dealings with the Jews
on this particular morning seems to have had one concern
only—to shift the responsibility for the affair to others.

This fact is ineradicable from the pages of the narrative.
We find it in his initial attempt to get the Jews to carry out
their own sentence. We find it in the thrice proclaimed public
acquittal of the Prisoner; we find it in the remission to
Herod; we find it supremely in that tense moment, when,
unable any longer to make himself heard above the tumult,
he washed his hands as a sign that he would have no part or
lot in it.

So in a member of Pilate's own household we discover the
fourth factor in the psychological parallelogram of personal
forces which brought about the death of Christ. The influence of Jesus upon the women of His day was profound,
and of surpassing interest. He took Mary Magdalene from
her native Magdala and made her His bond-slave for ever.
He took the sons and breadwinners away from women like
Salome and Mary the wife of Cleophas, yet they would have
died willingly for His cause, and did later endure unspeak-
able hardships on His account. He was the close and intimate
friend of cultured women like Mary and her sister Martha.
He had in Joanna a faithful and devoted follower in the very
household of Herod. Must we add Claudia to the circle of
His adherents?

In the sense of actual discipleship, no. But in the sense that
in some mysterious way she had come under the impress of
His moral influence and His commanding spiritual and
intellectual stature, I think we must say, yes. It was she who
stiffened the Roman instinct for justice in Pilate, at a moment
when he was tempted, from personal considerations, to
humour the prejudices of the Jewish camarilla, and commit

Jesus on their recommendation alone. It was she who was the author of that resplendent phase when the tyrant was seen for a few hours in the guise of a patient administrator anxious to weigh the truth to the last ounce. Let us not belittle this glowing if transient chapter in Pilate's chequered life.

While the stimulus lasted his handling of this difficult and perplexing case was wellnigh perfect. No juster hearing could any man have asked or obtained in any court of that far-off day. The restraining influence of one who clearly believed that Jesus was innocent is obviously upon it. It was only as the stimulus faded against the grinding and growing opposition of the Jewish party that the threat of Cæsar's intervention became paramount, and he ended as he intended to begin, by delivering the Prisoner into their hands.

So the battle of wills closed in the defeat of the Roman Procurator, and it was probably a sad and intensely irritated man who made his way back to the Imperial apartments of the Royal Palace. But we do not have to wait long for the repercussion.

A few hours later the Priests came back to him again. In his haste, or perhaps out of a coarse wish to turn the tables on his tormentors, he had written in three languages the immortal inscription: 'This is the King of the Jews.' They wanted him to alter it. He refused. 'What I have written I have written'—the real Pilate came out at last, when the supreme moment of his own personal and individual crisis had passed.

Chapter V

THE SITUATION ON FRIDAY
AFTERNOON

If we are to gain a real insight into the events which immediately followed the death of Christ we shall have to begin by studying carefully the situation as it probably existed about four o'clock on Friday afternoon.

Hitherto we have approached this subject almost exclusively from the official and priestly point of view. That point of view was extremely important in the earlier stages of the case. The prosecution was the Priests', and it was vital to our purpose to know what lay behind it. But with the achievement of their main object, these official representatives of Jewry recede temporarily into the background and a new group of people takes their place. It is with this group —the personal friends and adherents of Jesus—that we shall be chiefly concerned in the next two or three chapters. Let us begin by considering who these people were, and what the documents tell us with regard to them.

If we exclude Mary and Martha of Bethany, and their brother Lazarus, who, for certain reasons which we shall discuss later, are not heard of in connection with the final tragedy, we are left with a group of sixteen persons, all of whom are known to have belonged to the inner circle of Christ's personal supporters:

The eleven surviving Apostles.
Mary the Mother of Jesus.
Mary, the wife of Cleophas.
Salome, the wife of Zebedee.
Mary Magdalene.
Joanna, the wife of Chuza, Herod's steward.
To these should perhaps be added two men of a higher

social class, who, while not openly avowing discipleship, were apparently strongly sympathetic towards the cause of Christ—Joseph of Arimathea and the Councillor Nicodemus.

According to the narratives, every one of these eighteen persons was present in Jerusalem or its vicinity at this particular Feast. We have documentary track of them all. This is particularly important in the case of the women, because, as we shall see, their evidence carries special weight in certain contingencies which were shortly to arise.

Now the question which we have chiefly to consider here is this: In what way did the blow occasioned by the summary arrest and crucifixion of Christ fall upon this little group of people? What were the exact circumstances in which they realized what was on foot and how did they behave under the stress of events which not only brought death to their leader, but were destined profoundly to affect their own lives?

Fortunately we can answer this question for the disciples outright. There does not seem to be any reasonable doubt that full realization only came late on Thursday evening. The special solemnity of the words of Jesus during the supper in the upper room had doubtless prepared them for some undefined catastrophe. But it was probably only when Judas arrived with the armed contingent that the dastardly and terrible character of the betrayal came home to them. After a brief and futile attempt at resistance on the part of Peter, the majority of them appear to have fled. The night passed into the morning with Jesus in the hands of His captors and His most intimate followers scattered and terrified by what they had seen.

Before the day was more than an hour old, however, two of these men, Peter and John, reappear in the dangerous and highly compromising neighbourhood of the High Priest's house. It seems reasonable to assume that they entered the city by following closely on the heels of the arrest party. If we are to accept the accounts given to us of the arrest, it was a somewhat heterogeneous body which accompanied the officers of the Sanhedrin to the Garden of Gethsemane. Arrangements had doubtless been made at the gates to readmit this gathering on the return of the expedition, and it should not have been difficult in the darkness and general confusion, for Peter and John to have slipped in without their identity being recognized. Once inside the city gates they would probably follow the main body to the High Priest's house, where John's acquaintance with the portress seems to have served them in good stead.

With regard to the other nine disciples, I think it is very doubtful whether any of them slept in the city that night. They were evidently panic-stricken, and fled to avoid the possibility of arrest. Admitting the known fact that the rules governing the opening of the gates of the city after sundown were greatly relaxed during the feasts, when many pilgrims slept in booths on the surrounding hills, it seems very unlikely that men under a sudden impulse of fear would risk detection by seeking admission at such an unusual hour. It is far more likely that they took a quite different course which will be dealt with fully in a later chapter.

The women of the party were, therefore, in all human probability, cut off from direct knowledge and participation in this affair until at any rate the nocturnal phase of the trial of Jesus was over. It should not be forgotten that while news flies quickly in these days of newspapers and wireless installations, the conditions in Old Jerusalem were peculiar. The arrest of Jesus was not decided upon until very late the previous night when the majority of citizens had gone to bed. The return of the arrest party was probably made by the least frequented route, and there would be few stragglers in the Upper City at that hour. The circumstances favoured therefore that degree of secrecy so much desired by the Priests. When the gates opened at sunrise, and people began to pass in and out, rumours of the dramatic night proceedings doubtless began to circulate and a steadily growing stream of curious people probably made their way to the Upper City. But it seems to be implied in the narratives that anything like a wide or universal realization of what was taking place was delayed until later, when the great tragedy was being consummated.

We shall, therefore, be very near to the real truth in this

matter if we assume that the women of the party did not learn of the deadly and menacing turn which things had taken until early on Friday morning, either through the spread of rumours, or (as is more likely) by a hurried visit from Peter or John. To those who loved Jesus it would be a prime consideration to inform His mother at all costs.

If this be a reasonably accurate estimate of the position, it will be seen that the working efficiency of the party of Jesus in Jerusalem on Friday morning was reduced from sixteen persons to seven, of whom five were women. Had any of the nine remaining disciples succeeded in joining forces, either with Peter and John on the one hand or the women on the other, it seems incredible that we should not have heard of them.

The probability, too, that none of these nine men had yet returned is very greatly strengthened by the fact that the people we hear about in connection with the final scene at the Cross are drawn from this same group of seven persons. And they are all there except two[1] whose absence is justifiable. No anguish could prevent the Mother of such a Son from being present in the hour of His final agony, and we find Mary at the foot of the Cross. John, too, is there, anticipating in fact the sonship he was so soon to adopt. Mary, the wife of Cleophas, Salome, and Mary Magdalene are at a respectful distance.

All this is in accord with expectation. Even if the eleven disciples had been at hand to share the responsibilities and sorrows of that awful morning we should still have expected the women to have been present. The frailest women are drawn irresistibly to ministrations to the dying, even under conditions which will fray to tatters the nerves of strong men. But the picture of these solitary women and the disciple John 'standing by' in the hour of supreme crisis and doing what they could is very human and very true to life. If real history was ever written, surely it is this.

Consider now the events which immediately followed.

---

[1] Peter I take to have been in close retirement, an utterly humbled, repentant and broken man; while Joanna (in view of Herod's temporary residence in the city) was probably occupied with her official duties.

That Jesus Christ died upon the Cross, in the full physical sense of the term, even before the spear wound was inflicted by the Roman soldiery, seems to me to be one of the certainties of history.

All the accounts affirm it, and if the earliest record (St. Mark) is trustworthy, Pilate himself verified this point by direct inquiry of the centurion, before giving permission for the disposal of the body. No one seems to have questioned the fact at the time, or at any period during the lifetime of the eyewitnesses. It was reserved for the Rationalist Venturini at the beginning of the nineteenth century to advance the curious thesis that Jesus only swooned and recovered later in the cool of the rock-hewn grave. This theory has, however, been conclusively answered by Strauss and is dealt with in a later chapter.

Now all the four writers agree that, shortly after the death of Jesus, Pilate was approached by Joseph of Arimathea for permission to bury the body. Whatever doubts may attach, therefore, to other aspects of the tragedy, it seems indisputable that this man, a person of social distinction and even of official status, so far detached himself from the Priestly party as to seek permission to give the crucified Prisoner an honourable burial.

It is sometimes suggested that Joseph's motive in performing this act was to comply with the Jewish Law with regard to burial. I find it difficult to accept this suggestion in face of the evidence. There were *three bodies to be disposed of before sunset, not one*, and there is not the slightest trace of any solicitude on the part of Joseph for the two robbers. His sole motive and preoccupation seems to have been to pay a personal and individual respect to the remains of Jesus. So far from weakening this supposition, the few details given in the Gospels with regard to Joseph strengthen it. We are told that 'he consented not' in the Great Sanhedrin 'to the death of Christ'. St. Luke says: he 'was looking for the Kingdom of God'. St. John, rather more explicitly, but in quite different language, says 'he was a disciple, but secretly, for fear of the Jews'. But great events call forth heroic traits in the character of men, and when

Jesus was beyond the further pursuit of his enemies, Joseph seems to have risen to the level of his own secret aspirations. He had the courage to go to Pilate and ask for the body.

If we were left simply with the Synoptic Gospels we should be compelled to believe that Joseph of Arimathea acted in this matter entirely alone. St. John, however, contributes here an item of information, which, while unexpected, is by no means improbable. We are told that when Joseph had secured the permission of Pilate to bury the body, he brought Nicodemus with him—the man who, according to the same writer, came to Jesus by night.

I am not unmindful of the suspicion which exists in the minds of many competent critics with regard to facts which are reported solely by St. John, and upon which the Synoptists are silent. But the present case is surely exceptional. St. John is the only canonical writer who tells us anything about Nicodemus at all. Moreover, the two men had obviously much in common. Both were apparently drawn from the ruling class. Both held a secret but sincere regard for the personality of Jesus. That sooner or later they would come together was almost inevitable, and at what hour more likely than this, when the disfigured body of One whom they reverenced was about to be cast into a dishonourable grave! It was their last and only opportunity of rendering to Christ that outward allegiance which they had denied to Him in life.

Now it is necessary to remember that the effective Christian witnesses of what took place at this stage were in all human probability limited to the three women: Mary, the wife of Cleophas, Salome and Mary Magdalene. That the mother of Jesus herself collapsed when the end came may be regarded as certain. The Gospel record plainly implies it. The tortured heart and brain, wrought to the extremest pitch of anguish by the sufferings of the agonized figure on the Cross, would surely stand no more. Utter physical weakness and exhaustion would be the penalty she would pay for those few but awful hours at the foot of her dying and tortured Son. She would need all the loving and solicitous care of John to get her back through the rough crowds to their temporary home in Jerusalem.

But there is a very steady and consistent testimony in the Gospels that at least two of the other women stayed to see it through. They are expressly mentioned by the Synoptic writers, and in each case there is a curious suggestion of their viewing the burial from a little distance off, as though the circumstances forbade their giving any actual assistance. That seems to express accurately the probabilities of the situation. If the unanimous assertion of the four writers is true, that Joseph of Arimathea (a rich man and presumably a complete stranger to the women) conducted the burial, then their natural reticence—to say nothing of the difference in their social positions—would account sufficiently for the women standing aloof.

But there is one final consideration which must, I think, rank as one of the certainties of history. In no conceivable circumstances could Joseph of Arimathea have carried out what is recorded of him without assistance. *There must have been helpers.* The task of winding the body in a sheet eight feet long (the traditional Jewish practice) would have required at least two pairs of hands. The distance to be traversed from the hill of public execution to the garden grave could hardly have been short, and it must have required the strength of at least two grown men to carry a body the very wounds of which made it heavier and more difficult to handle. It is a very significant thing that while the Synoptists make no reference to Nicodemus, they are also silent upon the question of the helpers. Surely this is a case in which the presence of helpers is implied, and Nicodemus, being a complete stranger to the women, was possibly regarded as one of them.

It may seem a comparatively insignificant matter whether Joseph was assisted in his task of burying the body of Jesus or not, but, as we shall see, in a later chapter, it has an important bearing on the problem before us.

Such, then, in broad outline is how the Crisis overtook the friends of Jesus in Jerusalem on that ever-memorable Friday in human history. Looking at all these considerations squarely, we receive an impression of this far-off event which is not only true to the narratives, but which is palpably true to life. The broken fragments fit together and make a coherent and intelligible whole. It does not seem too big a claim to make that in this restrained and quiet narrative we have the irreducible certainties of a situation which, if unparalleled in its consequences, was very simple and very human in its essential details.

Thus Jesus, in the austere but exact phrasing of the English Prayer Book, 'suffered under Pontius Pilate, was crucified, dead, and buried. . . .' I have put dots in place of the famous context because as a young man I used to stop dead at this point in the English Church Service, set my teeth tightly, and refuse to utter another word. The reader will understand why.

But to-day I feel differently. I have wrestled with that problem and found it tougher than ever I could have conceived possible. It is easy to say that you will believe nothing that will not fit into the mould of a rationalist conception of the Universe. But suppose the facts won't fit into that mould? The utmost than an honest man can do is to undertake to examine the facts patiently and impartially, and to see where they lead him. That is what I propose to do in the following chapters.

Chapter VI

THIRTY-SIX HOURS LATER

By all the ordinary standards of human reasoning, the mystery attaching to the person of Christ ought to have terminated with His death and burial. That He really did die in the full physical meaning of that term we have already judged to be one of the certainties of history, and we have seen how a consistent and straightforward account is given of the steps which were taken to give the body a respectful burial. I cannot personally see anything in the accounts of the Crucifixion and burial which is not deeply and profoundly true to expectation. The whole thing reads like an actual, unvarnished, and even naïve transcript from real life. Yet directly we turn over the page to the events of the succeeding days we run into a situation which, were it not for the complete singularity of certain aspects of the problem, would be utterly unbelievable by any student acquainted alike with history and the conclusions of modern thought.

It is because I believe that there are things lying hidden beneath the surface of the narrative which must profoundly modify the construction we place upon it, that I will ask the reader to consider first the trend of events from about six o'clock on Friday afternoon to the setting out of the little party of women at dawn on Sunday morning.

It will be remembered that of the nine persons known to have been present in Jerusalem on Friday afternoon who were sympathetic to the cause of Christ, we were able definitely to trace *seven*. The apostle John was found with Mary the Mother of Jesus at the foot of the Cross, and, if the inferences we drew are correct, he left shortly after the final agony to escort his charge to a place of safety and retirement. The three women; Mary Magdalene; Mary, the wife of

Cleophas; and Salome, were also discovered in the neighbourhood of the Cross, while later in the afternoon Joseph of Arimathea and the Councillor Nicodemus appeared on their self-appointed mission to give an honourable burial to the body of Jesus.

Thus, seven out of the nine people are definitely accounted for. Of the two absentees, Peter's grief and shame at his panic-stricken denial of his Master will sufficiently explain his remaining in close retirement, while the ninth member of the group—the woman Joanna—turns up in connection with the expedition to the tomb on Sunday morning.

A moment's reflection will show, therefore, that what we may call the active and mobile section of the party of Jesus within the walls of Jerusalem was limited to the three women—Mary Magdalene; Mary, the wife of Cleophas; and Salome, supported, so far as her official duties would allow, by the woman Joanna.

It is only when we realize that these three or four women bore the whole brunt of the crisis which so suddenly descended upon the party of Jesus, carrying on bravely and doing of their own initiative what the situation seemed to demand, that we begin to see the tragic events of this particular week-end in all their naked realism and to discern the meaning of much which would otherwise remain obscure. For that these women did sustain the full impact of the crisis alone and cut off from effective communication with their friends save for such help as could be given by distracted Peter and preoccupied John, seems to be written plainly in the narratives.

Let us try to reconstruct the scene, taking as our guide the most ancient record, the Gospel of St. Mark. Fortunately the testimony of St. Mark, so far as our present inquiry is concerned, is very clear and definite. It will be remembered that in describing the final scene at the Crucifixion, he writes:

'There were also women beholding from afar: among whom were both Mary Magdalene, and Mary the mother of James the less and of Joses, and Salome.'

Then, after relating in the briefest possible manner the facts of the interment, St. Mark continues:

'And Mary Magdalene and Mary the mother of Joses beheld where he was laid.

'And when the sabbath was past, Mary Magdalene, and Mary the mother of James, and Salome, bought spices, that they might come and anoint him. And very early on the first day of the week, they come to the tomb when the sun was risen.'

Now there are two very interesting things which stand out from this narrative and demand attention.

1. The precedence which is given to Mary Magdalene, as though she were in some way the recognized leader and dominant personality of the group.
2. The curious disappearance of Salome during the actual interment of Jesus.

We may pass over for the moment the point with regard to Mary Magdalene. But the references to Salome are suggestive and throw real light upon the narrative. St. Mark is rather careful about his names and places. He explicitly names Salome as being present at the Crucifixion. He also mentions her as being one of the women who visited the tomb at dawn. Yet it was only the two Marys who stayed behind and 'beheld where he was laid'.

This pointed omission of Salome during the actual interment can hardly have been accidental. It must mean that the writer of St. Mark's Gospel wished to convey that Salome had gone away, presumably upon some pressing business.

What that business was can be inferred with a degree of probability so high as to amount almost to certainty. It should be remembered that Mary, the wife of Cleophas, and Salome were *cousins* and throughout their terrible ordeal, when companionship and mutual help meant so much, were acting in close concert with Mary Magdalene. Further, both women were related to Mary the Mother of Jesus, while Salome herself was the mother of the apostle John.

This devoted band of women must have had two intense preoccupations during the terrible closing hours of the

Crucifixion. The one was solicitude for their great leader who was passing through frightful tortures to His end. The other was an equally intense solicitude for their kinswoman, the Mother of Jesus herself. So long as life lingered in the body of Jesus the whole emotional field would be flooded with thoughts and solicitude for Him. But when release came at last with a great cry from the dying Man, the other preoccupation would assert itself.

We do not know, we cannot know, what earnest but fruitless attempts were made that day to keep Mary away from the Cross. She was no longer young, and the bloody scene of a triple crucifixion was no sight for an overstrained and utterly heart-broken woman. Personally, I think that the whole weight of the advice and entreaty of the little party must have been exerted against it. But the mother instinct was too strong. She insisted on being with her boy to the end; and who could deny her the right if she was determined to exercise it?

But I do not think that anyone outside the medical profession can gauge the physical risks she ran, or how near the heart-rending ordeal brought her to fatal seizure. The woman that John led away from that frightful scene was surely already half-fainting, dazed, and in less than half an hour, as fuller realization came, would surely collapse.

At a respectful distance from the Cross our three women are watching. As the great cry goes up it is clear that the end has come, and they see John leading the distracted Mother, first to the outskirts of the crowd, and then painfully and slowly citywards. A hurried consultation is held. Someone must go to the aid of the stricken woman, while the others do what they can for Jesus. Salome volunteers, for it is her son John who is leading the bereaved Mother home.

That, I take it, is the true reading of these events. It would have had to be inferred even if the Gospels contained no hint of it. But the language of St. Mark is to my mind conclusive.

Thus in the very earliest of the records, the record which is universally judged to be the closest in point of time to the events themselves, we get this vivid picture of a tiny remnant of the party of Jesus reeling under the shock of the Cruci-fixion, disposing their limited forces as best they could to meet unprecedented emergencies—Peter overwhelmed with remorse and shame remaining in strict retirement; John, with the aid of Salome, tending the stricken Mother now committed to their charge; Mary Magdalene and the other Mary, assisted as circumstances permitted by Joanna and Salome, making their tentative arrangements for paying the last tribute of love and friendship to their dead leader.

Such as I read it was the position just after sunset on Friday, when the beginning of the Sabbath set a limit to any further operations at the tomb of Jesus. It is all very human and very true to life. It is the kind of situation which all of us, and especially every woman, can understand.

*   *   *   *   *

Now it is one of the unmistakable inferences from the narratives that this particular poise of events persisted practically unchanged throughout the ensuing Sabbath, and that when the women retired to rest on Saturday evening it was with the definite intention of rising early the following morning to go to the tomb.

Usually, when one is trying to reconstruct a scene, after an interval of centuries, and, as in this case, with records which are admittedly brief, one has to rely upon the cumulative effect of small details to discover the key facts of the situa-tion. But in the present instance the records themselves are explicit. All the four writers testify that the time of the visit was about daybreak—that is to say, much before the hour when ordinary people would be about. St. Mark's statement is that it was: '*very early . . .* when the sun was risen'. St. Matthew says: '*as it began to dawn*'. St. Luke describes it as: '*at early dawn*'. The writer of the Fourth Gospel (in this case an important witness) gives it as '*early, while it was yet dark*'.

I cannot personally find any grounds, in the slight varia-tion in these statements as to whether the sun had actually risen or not, for doubting the central fact in these quotations.

One must not overlook the fact that the sun rises very quickly in Southern latitudes, that women are specially prone to unforeseen delays when engaged in joint expeditions, and that while they doubtless rose when it was still dark, the sun was probably some degrees up by the time they got to the tomb. In any case, the unanimous witness of the four documents is that it was *early*, and at the first available moment after the Sabbath.

So much for the element of time. Let us now consider the personnel of the expedition. If we put the four records side by side and select what it emphatically asserted in common by them all we find them in complete agreement about one thing, viz. that somewhere about the time that the sun was due to rise Mary Magdalene arose and went to the sepulchre.

This minimum statement of the facts is contained in a passage in the Fourth Gospel which has perhaps been more widely scrutinized and discussed than any other passage in literature:

'Now on the first day of the week cometh Mary Magdalene early, while it was yet dark, unto the tomb, and seeth the stone taken away from the tomb. She runneth therefore, and cometh to Simon Peter, and to the other disciple, whom Jesus loved, and saith unto them, They have taken away the Lord out of the tomb, and we know not where they have laid him.'

What inferences are we to draw from this passage? Did Mary Magdalene go alone to the sepulchre? The question is a vital one, and we should think well before returning too confident an answer. For my own part, after reading the passage through again and again, I cannot help feeling that if the writer of the Fourth Gospel had realized at the time that this question of the women was going to become a matter of deep interest to millions of readers in succeeding centuries, he would have modified the literary construction of this particular sentence so as to remove the obvious *non sequitur* of the plural 'we'.

It is not the custom of the writer of the Fourth Gospel to be intentionally obscure or confusing when describing matters of fact. On the contrary, his work contains examples of some of the most lucid and vivid descriptive writing in literature. He commands a literary technique capable of expressing the most delicate nuances of meaning and he almost invariably uses it to produce an impression of pellucid clarity.

But in this passage—whether from a momentary inattention or because the subject of Mary's friends did not seem to him important, I know not—he has achieved one of the outstanding literary examples of obscurity in the Gospels. He begins by describing Mary's departure for the tomb at a time when few people would be about unless they had risen with the intention of accompanying her. He describes her as running back in a state of great excitement to tell Peter and John, and he records what is clearly a deeply imprinted recollection of her breathless and historic utterance: 'They have taken away the Lord, and we know not where they have laid him.'

Why this incomprehensible 'we' if it was not part of his understanding of the matter that Mary did not go unattended and that she was reporting what she had found, or rather failed to find, in company with others?

Considerable light is thrown on this matter by a study of the famous fragment of the so-called Gospel of Peter. The writer of this fragment also gives supreme prominence to the action of Mary Magdalene, but he adds a phrase which would have removed entirely the obscurity in St. John:

'Now early on the Lord's day Mary Magdalene, a disciple of the Lord, which, being afraid because of the Jews, for they were inflamed with anger, had not performed at the sepulchre of the Lord those things which women are accustomed to do unto them that die and are beloved of them—*took with her* the women her friends and came unto the tomb where he was laid.'

Here we get part of what is almost certainly the true picture: Mary Magdalene as the prime mover in all this strange business of the surreptitious visit to the tomb, but accompanied, if only for safety and for decency's sake, by her own chosen and intimate friends, women of wider experience and maturer years.

Thirty-six Hours Later

If we turn now to the accounts in the three Synoptic Gospels we are immediately impressed by their solidarity with this point of view. All three writers say with the utmost certainty and definiteness that Mary, the wife of Cleophas, went with Mary to the tomb. St. Mark says that Salome accompanied them, St. Luke mentions Joanna as the third member of the party. Having regard to the solemnity and uniqueness of the occasion, is it not at least possible that all four women went?

The more one considers the peculiar circumstances of this historic moment in the lives of these simple people, the more certain does it seem that, could we go back to Jerusalem in the dim dawn of that memorable Sunday, we should see Mary Magdalene and the other Mary, accompanied either by Salome or Joanna, trudging sorrowfully through the narrow unlighted streets of the Lower City on their way to pay the last tribute of respect to their dead leader.

*   *   *   *   *

It is important that we should satisfy ourselves beyond any reasonable possibility of doubt as to who it was that first visited the sepulchre on Sunday morning because the moment we allow these women to approach the burial-place of Christ we reach the startling abnormality that, according to their report, the body was no longer there. This fact is stated or implied so definitely in the records that it compels us to face sharply and at once a phase of the history which must rest basically upon the evidence and upon nothing else.

The first thing which arrests attention in this connection is that the object with which these women visited the tomb was a perfectly natural one, and the hour at which they did so was consistent with their purpose. It was widely accepted in the East that decomposition of the body of a dead person set in on or about the third day after death. It was necessary, therefore, to perform the rites which the women had in view at the earliest possible moment consistent with the observance of the Sabbath. That moment was undoubtedly at sunrise on Sunday morning. They would clearly choose an early hour to avoid publicity. They could hardly go before sunrise because it would be dark, and possibly also because the city gates would not be open.

We are therefore very amply within the field of historic probability when we picture this little party of three or four women approaching the tomb in the dim dawn of Sunday morning. But this is not the only fact recorded in the Gospels which looms solid and very real through the mists of time. I mean the preoccupation of the women with the difficulties they were likely to experience with the stone which, according to all the documents, was placed against the entrance to the grave.

The question as to how they were to remove this stone must of necessity have been a source of considerable perplexity to the women. Two of them at least had witnessed the interment and knew roughly how things stood. The stone, which is known to have been large and of considerable weight, was their great difficulty. When, therefore, we find in the earliest record, the Gospel of St. Mark, the words: 'Who shall roll us away the stone from the door of the tomb?' we can hardly avoid feeling that this preoccupation of the women with the question of the stone is not only a psychological necessity of the problem, but a definitely historical element in the situation right up to the moment of their arrival at the grave.

Now to anyone actuated by a desire, not to score points, but to arrive at the historic truth, it will be obvious that the fragments of recollection which have reached us as to what actually happened during the next few minutes reflect an experience of no ordinary kind. It is not as though the different accounts agree. If they did we should have to approach the problem from a different angle. But they make no attempt or pretence of agreeing, even though the earliest version of what happened was before both St. Matthew and St. Luke when they wrote, and all three Synoptic Gospels were common property when the author of the Fourth Gospel produced his work. The one thing which seems to be certain is that on arrival at the tomb, they received a shock for which they were totally unprepared.

The essence of their discovery was that the tomb had in some way been disturbed and that contrary to their expectations the body of Jesus was no longer there. St. Luke summarizes the consistent testimony of the Synoptic writers upon this point when he says: 'they found not the body'. But as though to underscore the deeply imbedded character of this tradition we have that immensely significant passage in the Gospel according to St. John—a passage so outspoken and diverse from the Synoptic versions that even the uncritical reader must be arrested by it:

'She' (Mary Magdalene) 'runneth therefore, and cometh to Simon Peter, and to the other disciple, whom Jesus loved, and saith unto them, They have taken away the Lord out of the tomb, and we know not where they have laid him.'

I do not wish to influence unduly the opinion of anyone who feels that when it comes to choosing between the Synoptic writers and the writer of the Fourth Gospel about a matter of historic fact the earlier writers have the prior claim to acceptance. But I am bound to say that, coming where it does, this passage impresses me profoundly. It is like a clear shaft of sunlight piercing the mists of this memorable dawn.

Unless, therefore, we are prepared to throw overboard the whole *corpus* of the surviving literary evidence, a course which I am convinced no honest and critical reader of this book will suggest, we are driven to the conclusion that when these women reached the tomb they really did receive the impression that the body had gone. I think also that it is a reasonable inference that, coming as it did at dawn, under somewhat eerie conditions, and to minds utterly unprepared for it, this discovery by itself was calculated to produce a condition bordering upon hysteria. Particularly will this appear to be the case when we remember that two at least of the women were no longer young. We have no means of knowing the age of Joanna, but Mary the wife of Cleophas and Salome must have been approaching, if they had not already reached their fifth decade.

This point may not seem at first sight to be of much

importance, but psychologically its significance is considerable. These women must have felt and acted very much as
a similar group of women might feel and act to-day if confronted suddenly and at an unnaturally early hour by an
equally unexpected phenomenon in Kensal Green Cemetery.
The first and immediate effect would be one of stupor, followed quickly by an urgent sense of the necessity of immediate counsel and help. If, therefore, as seems very
probable, Mary Magdalene, the youngest and most active
member of the group, volunteered to run quickly back to the
city to tell the disciples Peter and John, leaving the older
women to follow at their own pace, we should have a situation which corresponds closely with the version given in
the Fourth Gospel and which accounts satisfactorily for
Mary's breathless employment of the plural 'we'.

Whether we may make this further inference or not is a
legitimate matter for future study, but the central fact in this
strange episode does not seem to be susceptible of doubt.
These women planned to perform a certain service to their
late Master at the earliest moment consistent with the observance of the Sabbath. In accordance with their purpose
they arose very early on Sunday morning and went to the
tomb. But the supremely important historical fact is that
this service was never rendered. Whatever else happened in
Joseph's garden that morning, the evidence is that the
women failed to find Him and that according to their report
the body was no longer there.

Chapter VII

ON THE BEHAVIOUR OF TWO SISTERS
AND THE MEN WHO FLED IN THE NIGHT

Before we can consider what these facts mean, and especially what validity attaches to the various explanations which have been brought forward to account for them, it is necessary to complete that general picture of the historic background which has hitherto engaged our thought.

We saw in a preceding chapter that the sudden and unexpected arrest of Jesus in the Garden of Gethsemane late on Thursday night split the little party of His personal adherents into two distinct groups. Throughout the preceding chapters we have been studying in some detail what took place in connection with the smaller of these fragments, the one which was, as it were, marooned or temporarily isolated in Jerusalem itself. We have given comparatively little thought to the larger fragment outside. Yet the behaviour of this larger fragment is one of the essential factors of the problem. Is there anything in the documents which throws any light upon this important question?

It will serve to clarify our thought if we remember that there are really *two* missing groups of people which have to be accounted for. There are the nine disciples who are reported to have fled at the arrest, but there are also the sisters Mary and Martha of Bethany, whose absence from the Crucifixion and burial is one of the most notable and significant features of the narratives. Here are two sisters who were devoted heart and soul to Jesus. Their restful home was one of the few luxuries He ever allowed Himself. It was probably from their house that He stepped out on the last morning He was to see as a free man. Yet when the blow fell and every ounce of comfort was needed by His stricken supporters, these two homely and devoted women slip utterly out of the picture. There must be some solid and historic reason for this, and it is our task, if possible, to find it.

It is usually a sound inference when two or more unusual features emerge in an otherwise normal and intelligible situation, to assume that there is some connection between them. In the present instance there are special reasons for suspecting it. We must never forget that throughout the troubled five days which preceded the arrest, Jesus and His companions had made their home at Bethany. I have sometimes speculated as to whether the domestic arrangements in the house of the two sisters permitted of accommodating the thirteen persons who constituted the party. Probably they did not, in which case Jesus and possibly one or two of the elder apostles stayed in the house, while the other disciples found temporary lodgings nearby.

In any case the evidence is that the whole party slept in the village throughout the week, making the three-mile journey to and from Bethany each day. Further, with the exception of Judas Iscariot, who knew otherwise, the probabilities are that the disciples fully expected to return to Bethany as usual on Thursday night. That mysterious lingering in the Garden long after the usual time for retiring must have been very perplexing to them, and as the hour steadily approached midnight the minds of the two sisters also must have become the prey of anxiety.

With these facts before us let us go back to the scene in the Garden of Gethsemane. All the accounts agree in suggesting that the party sent by the priests to effect the arrest was too large to admit of them walking or marching abreast. Even on the road leading from the city gate to the junction of the Bethany road and the mountain track over Olivet they would probably form an irregular column stretching roughly some twenty yards along the road. We have to think of this irregular and motley aggregation of rather excited men arriving at the entrance of the Garden and deploying through the trees to the place where Jesus was, the torch-bearers with Judas in their midst coming first, accompanied by the Temple Guards, and these in turn followed by the miscellaneous body of 'witnesses' and other persons assembled at short notice in the city.

The arrest would, of course, be made immediately Judas had identified Jesus, and Peter had probably already struck the blow at the servant of the High Priest before the rear of the arrest party had closed in or knew precisely what was going on. There would probably be a good deal of shouting and confusion as, with the torches held aloft in the centre of the open space between the trees, the officers of the Sanhedrin tied the hands of Jesus behind His back. In the meantime the rest of the expedition must have closed in upon the little knot of men surrounding the Prisoner.

It is no part of our present purpose to inquire how it was that Peter and John came to be separated from their comrades and to get into the city unrecognized. It seems probable, however, that, standing close to Jesus as Peter undoubtedly was, and with the available space between the trees rapidly filling, both Peter and John became involved in the crowd in such a way as to make withdrawal conspicuous. In the very dim light, and with the torches flickering uncertainly ahead, it may have been not only prudent, but the simplest way of achieving their purpose, to go on with the crowd, relying upon the obviously motley character of the gathering to secure their admission unchallenged at the gates. It is only in some accidental and unpremeditated fashion such as this that we can imagine them having the hardihood to risk detection by entering the city.

If this is what actually happened then we have precisely the conditions already postulated as obtaining in Jerusalem on the following morning.

But our main interest is at present with the other nine disciples. Before we can even remotely contemplate the possibility of these men fleeing away there and then to Galilee, as Dr. Lake suggests in a theory which we shall discuss later, we must look at this situation very closely and especially at the springs of their conduct.

People usually fly in panic when some dreaded personal

disaster is very near, very pressing, and when there is no time for calmer reflection or the invention of resource. In this case the danger was at one time very close, but the disciples could not have run many yards through the thicket before the realities of the situation would be forced upon them.

In the first place, if the Garden occupied the site which tradition has always assigned to it, it lay at the foot of the hill of Olivet. The arrest party must have entered it by a gate opening on to the main Jericho road. Anyone fleeing therefore from such a party and desiring to avoid observation would do so in the direction *opposite* to that from which the party had come—that is to say, up the sloping side of Olivet and towards Bethany. Every step that they took would bring them higher up and in a position of advantage over the Garden below.

Fortunately for the disciples, the extent of their possible danger was clearly indicated. If anyone was searching for them among the trees below the fact would be indicated by the visible trail of the torches. Every move in the game would be apparent, and the disciples were in a position of unparalleled advantage. They had only to watch for an approaching light and keep it at a distance.

But it seems obvious that nothing of this kind took place. After the lapse of a few moments the whole arrest party appears to have returned to Jerusalem. The retreating lights of the torch-bearers would be clearly visible as the party wound its way to the appointed entrance. Whatever immediate danger there was to the remaining disciples retreated with those lights. Nothing further would happen until daylight came.

This is the common-sense view of the matter, and there is no logical or visible reason for it being otherwise. Given this period of respite, what would be the psychological state and position of the disciples? How would they behave? What urgent considerations would press for solution?

No one can possibly answer these questions with full knowledge and certainty, but we can hazard a guess and correct it by our observations later. It seems to me that if the disciples stopped to take stock of their position, one fact must have presented itself to them in a very alarming light— *the fact that both Peter and John were missing*. They would put the worst possible construction upon this. They could not be expected to know or foresee the peculiarly fortuitous circumstances in which these two men probably gained entrance to the city. Seen from their side of the shield, the absence of Peter and John—their total failure to respond to the calls of the comrades—would assume a most sinister significance. They would probably infer that they had been arrested, and that only their own promptitude in retreating at the critical moment had saved them from a similar fate.

This would, I think, effectually deter them from making any immediate attempt to get into the city. On the other hand, if (as they assumed) John and Peter had been taken prisoners, the position of the women, unprotected and exposed to the full blast of the Priests' hostility and the popular frenzy, would be very serious. That was a point which must undoubtedly be taken into account. Beyond this, if there were no other data available, we could perhaps hardly go. We should have to leave the nine missing disciples on the hill of Olivet, and admit that as to what happened thereafter, there was no clue.

But we have still to explain that other remarkable fact— the simultaneous disappearance from the narratives of Mary and Martha. Are these two circumstances connected? Will one given set of conditions explain both? What combination of circumstances will account for the absence of these two women from Jerusalem during the terrible hours which preceded and followed the Crucifixion? How is it that when every other woman of the inner circle of Christ's companionship seems to have been engaged and indeed deeply immersed in the affair, Mary and Martha, to whom He owed so much, are so strikingly missing?

A great deal of light is thrown upon this matter when we remember the strategic position of Bethany. This little village, nestling on the other side of Olivet, was, as it were, the sentinel of Jerusalem on the main Jericho road. Anyone coming from the north, up the steep ravine from Jericho immortalized by Jesus in the story of the Good Samaritan, had to pass through Bethany. Conversely, in going from Jerusalem to the north the traveller had to pass through it.

This fact has a number of important bearings upon our problem. In the first place, it means that if the disciples really had set off to go to Galilee they would have had to pass within a few yards of the home of Mary and Martha at which, or near to which, they had been staying for the past five days. Assuming they got so far, with the clear evidence of the darkness to show that they were not followed, is it conceivable that they would not have gone in to break the appalling news to the sisters and to seek their counsel and help?

But there are a number of other reasons why the disciples would, in all human probability, make for Bethany.

1. Such belongings as they possessed (and it is not to be imagined that they would travel without some simple kind of impedimenta) must have been at Bethany as their temporary home.

2. Mary and Martha, as intimate friends of Jesus, would need warning of the dangerous turn which events had just taken. There was time for them to fly too, if flight was really necessary.

3. If the women actually in the city realized what was going on and found it prudent to leave Jerusalem, they would fly first to Bethany, for through Bethany their course lay.

Thus the peculiar position of the village, combined with the fact that the home of Mary and Martha was an obvious rendezvous for both groups of possible fugitives, marked it out as the place to which the disciples would almost instinctively go.

Whether, therefore, we hold that these nine men set out at once to go to Galilee, or whether we hold that they were of the sterner stuff which would at least make an effort to rescue their womenfolk, or whether we picture the situation as merely one in which nine tired men in urgent need of rest went to the nearest and most likely place, we bring these men within a short time of the arrest to Bethany.

Let us now look at the matter from the inner side of the little home at Bethany. As we have already seen, the situation described in the Gospels implies that the two sisters were expecting Jesus to return on Thursday evening, and, as the hours went by and He did not come, they would naturally become alarmed and anxious. Had the night passed without any news of Him at all, it seems certain that one at least of the sisters would have journeyed to Jerusalem the next morning, when contact would have been established between the two groups. In that case we should probably have heard of Mary or Martha of Bethany (perhaps both) being present at the Crucifixion and burial.

We can find, however, nothing even remotely suggesting this in the Gospels. The complete silence of all the records with reference to the Bethany sisters, particularly as regards the women's project and subsequent visit to the tomb, is extremely suggestive and challenging. It can only mean that the conditions prevailing in Bethany either prevented news of the tragic denouement reaching them or that for sufficiently good reasons they refrained from attempting to join their friends within the walls.

That this is what happened seems to be indicated by the peculiar quality and atmosphere of the records. If only two or three of these worn-out and unhappy men made their way in the darkness to the little home at Bethany, can we not imagine what would have taken place?

We must make allowance, I think, for the obviously shaken nerve of the disciples. Jesus had just been arrested by the Temple Guard and by order of the Priests. John and Peter (in their view) had also been arrested. The mood of the people was violently hostile. All this would be told, losing nothing of its menace by reason of the uncanny hour at which it was related. On the other side the women were impressionable, and knowing nothing of the true state of affairs would readily form an idea of the situation, darker than even the facts warranted. Whichever way they looked at it the future was full of immediate menace. What was going on behind the distant walls of Jerusalem? Perhaps even then the traitor Judas was preparing to lead another party at daybreak to complete the arrest. While the valleys around Olivet were being independently searched, Bethany would not be overlooked. They might even arrest the sisters as being implicated in the matter.

These are thoughts which would almost inevitably present themselves to their minds. But there were other considerations. *The mothers of three of these nine men* were still in Jerusalem exposed to dangers and possibilities which were uncertain but not the less real on that account. Would they get warning of their peril in time? If so, at any moment they too might knock at the door of that little house.

Of course, with history to guide us we know that the situation within the city was curiously different. We know that Peter and John were not arrested. We can see now that the Priests were satisfied when they secured Jesus, for it was Him they feared. But, given the flight of the disciples in obvious panic to Bethany, either as the first stage of the journey to Galilee, or as the most obvious sanctuary for the moment, the psychological atmosphere in that little home must have been roughly as we have described it. Uncertainty, apprehension, and fear for the personal safety of everyone connected with Jesus must have been its dominant note.

The following morning would bring no amelioration of this state—rather the coming of daylight would intensify it. Anything might happen and at any moment. The very worst was to be feared. It is curious to think that all the time Jesus was passing through the final and harrowing stages of His public trial, and while their supposed enemies were deeply obsessed with other things, this little group of people was probably labouring under the gravest apprehensions.

It is curious also to reflect that by the very nature of the circumstances they would tend to be cut off from knowledge of what was going on. In the ordinary way and at normal times there was a certain traffic between Jerusalem and Bethany by which news of what was taking place in the city would be received in two or three hours. But a judicial execution of the greatest Teacher the city had seen within living memory was a sensation of no ordinary kind. The square of Pilate's Court and the road to Calvary were an irresistible magnet, and the normal traffic between Jerusalem and Bethany would on that account be temporarily stayed.

Not until the great cry had gone up and the vast crowds poured back into the town is it probable that any real news of what was transpiring in Jerusalem percolated out to the surrounding villages, and by that time the sun was setting and the Sabbath was at hand.

Such, as I conceive it, was the most probable situation during those confused and dramatic hours when Jesus paid the great penalty. It accords with the clear teaching of the records, and it resolves what must otherwise remain utterly inexplicable and obscure. I submit it tentatively and with respect as a possible solution.

Chapter VIII

BETWEEN SUNSET AND DAWN

It is strange that there is no escaping the clock in all this baffling story of the closing phase of the life of Jesus.

We saw in an earlier chapter how the inexorable pressure of events precipitated the arrest, forced the hands of the authorities, prolonged the hour of the preliminary hearing, and modified profoundly the character of the Roman trial. It is as though everything in this affair was done under the lash of an invisible taskmaster, from whose decree there was no appeal. So now, whether we realize it at first or not, we shall find the problem steadily narrowing itself down to an investigation of what was happening just outside the walls of Jerusalem about 1,900 years ago between sunset on a certain Saturday and the first streaks of dawn on the following morning. Let us begin by considering in some detail the various hypotheses which have been put forward to account for the facts.

There is, of course, one suggestion which few readers of this book will expect to be argued seriously. I mean the suggestion, so widely circulated in apostolic times, that the disciples themselves had stolen or abducted the body. I do not propose to devote any considerable amount of space to testing the historical accuracy of this charge because the verdict has been anticipated by the almost universal sense and feeling of mankind. So far as I know there is not a single writer whose work is of critical value to-day who holds that there is even a case for discussion. We know these eleven men pretty well by their subsequent actions and writings. Somehow they are not built that way. There is no trace of the daring sort of ringleader who would have had the imagination to plan a *coup* like that and to carry it through without detection. Even if it had been possible, and the disciples the men to do it, the subsequent history of Christianity would have been different. Sooner or later, someone who knew the facts would have 'split'.

Further, no great moral structure like the Early Church, based as it was upon lifelong persecution and personal suffering, could have reared its head upon a statement which every one of the eleven apostles knew to be a lie. I have asked myself many times, would Peter have been a party to a deception like that, would John, would Andrew, would Philip or Thomas? Whatever the explanation of these extraordinary events may be, we may be certain that it was not that.

We are left, therefore, with the problem of the vacant tomb still unsolved. Can we get any light by exploring the various other explanations which have been advanced?

There are, in the main, six independent lines of critical approach to this matter. Four of them assume the vacancy of the tomb as an historic fact, while the others take the extremer view that the story is either entirely apocryphal or that the tomb was not investigated under the conditions described in the Gospels. Very briefly these hypotheses may be summarized as follows:

1. That Joseph of Arimathea secretly removed the body to a more suitable resting-place.
2. That the body was removed by order of the Roman Power.
3. That the body was removed by the Jewish authorities to prevent the possible veneration of the tomb.
4. That life was not really extinct, and that Jesus recovered in the cool of the grave.
5. That the women mistook the grave in the uncertain light.
6. That the grave was not visited at all and that the story about the women was a later accretion.

This is a very wide field of presuppositions and, so far as I know, includes every serious alternative to the Gospel thesis which has been put forward. Let us look at them in turn for a few moments.

1. That Joseph of Arimathea removed the Body
At first sight the suggestion that the man who, by

universal consent, begged the body of Jesus from the Roman Procurator, might himself have removed it for private reasons to another place, is one which seems to carry considerable weight.

The inferences drawn by a number of writers from the rather slender details given in the Gospels are that the tomb was probably purchased by Joseph for his own use, that its proximity to the scene of the Crucifixion suggested its temporary employment during the Sabbath, and that at the earliest possible moment Joseph would wish to remove the remains to a more permanent resting-place. All this is very understandable and, if the theory stood alone, it would present a quite remarkable and convincing aspect of self-consistency and strength. But we cannot leave a serious historical hypothesis in this state. It has to be worked out and superimposed upon the situation which it attempts to explain. The far, as well as the near consequences have to be explored and by its power to satisfy the whole of these conditions it must finally be judged.

Now a closer examination of this hypothesis reveals certain weaknesses and inconsistencies which affect its probability very gravely. In the first place the hour required for this supposititious removal (necessarily between the close of the Sabbath and the first sign of dawn) is in itself a rather strange time for a respected leader of the people to choose for a perfectly legitimate operation which could have been performed much better and more expeditiously at the break of day. It should never be forgotten that upon this theory Joseph of Arimathea and the little party of women were independently and quite unknown to each other planning to perform a service which would bring them to the tomb at the earliest possible moment consistent with the observance of the Sabbath. Having regard to the difficulties presented by the darkness that moment was unquestionably the break of day. Theoretically, therefore, Mary Magdalene and her friends upon reaching the tomb ought to have come upon the party of Joseph already at work.

There is no trace, however, of this dramatic meeting

taking place. We are compelled, therefore, to put the supposed removal further back into the night. We have to think of a party of men operating with lamps or torches, working under the maximum difficulties, picking their way through the unlighted regions beyond the city wall, carrying a heavy body, probably for some considerable distance, and depositing it in another grave. We have to think of them going to the trouble of removing all the grave-clothes first, leaving these in the tomb and removing the naked body to its destination. And we have to regard them as either forgetting to close the door of the old tomb, or not wishing for the moment to waste time by doing so.

Let us try to see the full force and weight of this particular reconstruction of the scene. I can imagine someone saying: 'Are we not here on the track of reality? Granted that dawn would have been the *ideal* time for this operation, but events may have determined otherwise. News flies quickly in proximity to a great national high road and Joseph may have feared that a task requiring at least two hours for its accomplishment might draw a large and dangerous crowd if undertaken after sunrise. May it not be that he really did carry out the preliminaries under cover of darkness and that when Mary Magdalene and her party arrived at the tomb, the party had already left for the locality of the permanent burial-place?'

This view of the matter possesses in a remarkable degree the required consistency with the records. It explains the surprise of the women on finding the great stone rolled away. It accounts for the tomb being discovered to be vacant. It agrees profoundly with Mary Magdalene's breathless message to the two disciples: 'They have taken away the Lord, and we know not where they have laid him!' If there were no other conditions to be satisfied, this would be the supremely convincing and naturalistic explanation. But again no theory, however plausible and convincing at first sight, can stand alone. It must fit the big facts of the situation as well as the little. And it is with the big facts that no conceivable adjustment seems to be possible.

There are two ways of regarding Joseph of Arimathea consistently with the narratives. Either he was:

(*a*) A secret follower or disciple of Jesus who seriously desired to perform openly this service to one whose leadership he had hesitated to acknowledge during life; or

(*b*) A pious member of the Sanhedrin who was only concerned with the fulfilment of the Jewish Law which enjoined burial of the crucified prisoner before sunset.

A great deal has been made of the second possibility, chiefly by those who are anxious to show cause for Joseph's supposed reluctance to allow the body of Jesus to remain in his own tomb. It seems to me, however, that there is one insuperable difficulty in the way of its acceptance. The Jewish Law which enjoined burial before sunset applied equally to the two thieves, and there is no suggestion that Joseph occupied himself with or even gave a thought to the remains of these two men. Now this is remarkable, because all three cases, involving as they did the capital sentence, came within the Roman jurisdiction. It was quite as necessary to obtain Pilate's permission in the case of the two thieves as it was in that of Jesus. No doubt the Priests did later obtain official authority to deal with these two men, and their bodies were probably cast into the common grave, but this was clearly after Joseph of Arimathea had made his own personal and independent request. The fact that Joseph did make this isolated application to Pilate shows that he was not acting in an official or representative sense. In any case, why should an honourable Councillor and a member of the Great Sanhedrin have undertaken with his own hands a menial task which could more appropriately have been left to the civil guard?

Secondly, there are very definite indications in the apocryphal literature that the Priests were very angry with Joseph of Arimathea and summoned him before the Council. There would have been no occasion for such anger if he had acted merely at their behest, but very good reasons for it if he has stultified their collective action in the eyes of the people and of Pilate himself, by giving to the body of

Jesus an honourable and respectful burial. Finally there is the explicit statement in St. Matthew's Gospel that Joseph was a disciple, and in St. Luke that he had not consented to their counsel and deed.

These considerations, taken together, seem to suggest that Joseph really was a sympathizer with Jesus who, stirred to the depths of his being by the illegality and fanaticism of what had been done, decided to give openly an honourable burial to the Great Teacher. With this object he went expressly to Pilate to beg the body, and with this object he chose his own tomb.

Now directly we accept this view of Joseph of Arimathea, we admit also a whole circle of ideas which are inseparable from it. In the first place it is extremely unlikely that in such circumstances Joseph would have wished to remove the body of Jesus at all. If he took the action recorded of him in the Gospels he compromised and even destroyed his social standing with the official and ruling caste. By that one act he threw in his lot irrevocably with the party of Jesus. He would hardly have adopted a bold and courageous course like that if he had not held Jesus in deep love and veneration. To one in his position, having made at long last the sacrifice he had hesitated to make during the living ministry, the thought that the revered leader and martyr rested in his own tomb would have been an imperishable consolation—the one hallowed recollection which would brighten the sad memories of his declining days. The more closely we consider this action of Joseph of Arimathea the more we get the impression of a man acting upon an inner compulsion to seize the last fleeting opportunity to align himself with the cause of Jesus before it was too late. Would he have incurred the penalties inseparable from his action— the contempt of his old associates, the deep hostility of the Priesthood, the ignominy of declaring himself a follower of the discredited and crucified Prophet—and have been willing within thirty-six hours to part with the glory? I think not. Overwhelmingly psychology is against it.

But there is another and even more cogent reason for thinking that Joseph was not responsible for the removal of the body. Within seven weeks at latest the disciples were back in Jerusalem declaring with the utmost certainty and conviction that Jesus had risen from the dead. If Joseph had made a perfectly legitimate removal of the body and (to avoid a popular demonstration) had done so in the middle of the night before Mary and her friends arrived at the Garden, the true facts of the matter must have been quite easily accessible to the Priests. After all, another tomb had to be found, and at least two or three helpers were required to carry the body. Why then, when all Jerusalem was seething with the Christian controversy, did they not simply tell the truth and thus give an effective quietus to the rumours due to the disappearance of the body?

Finally, and this to my mind carried conclusive weight, we cannot find in the contemporary records any trace of a tomb or shrine becoming the centre of veneration or worship on the ground that it contained the relics of Jesus. This is inconceivable if it was ever seriously stated at the time that Jesus was really buried elsewhere than in the vacant tomb. Rumour would have asserted a hundred supposititious places where the remains really lay, and pilgrimages innumerable would have been made to them.

Strange though it may appear, the only way in which we can account for the absence of this phenomenon is the explanation offered in the Gospels, viz. that the tomb was known, was investigated a few hours after the burial, and that the body had disappeared.

2 and 3. *That the Authorities (Jewish or Roman) removed the Body*

It will be convenient to take these two suggested solutions together, since the situation created by them is not markedly different from that which we have been considering.

It is no doubt possible, even at this distance of time, to suggest reasons why the body of Jesus might have been moved officially either by the Roman or the Jewish power, though the intrinsic probability of such a proceeding seems to be slight. Pilate was a very obstinate man, as his curt refusal to alter the terms of the inscription shows. He was clearly glad of any excuse to be rid of this painful incident, and if a Jew of substance desired and was granted the necessary permission to take charge of and bury the body, what more need have been done? With the Procurator in the mood in which he apparently then was, it would have required some exceedingly strong arguments to have induced him to alter his decision even at the instance of the Jewish power.

There is, of course, a very persistent tradition, both in the Gospels and the apocryphal writings, that the Jews did go to Pilate with a request. I shall deal with the very singular but important question of the guards in a later chapter. But the whole point of this tradition is to the effect that what the Priests are said to have sought of Pilate was not permission to remove the body, but to *prevent* it from being removed or stolen. There is not the slightest hint or suggestion in the earlier extant writings, apocryphal or otherwise, that the Priests ever contemplated changing the burial-place, while there are a number of distinct statements that they were concerned lest some unauthorized person should abduct the body.

But the whole case for the supposed official removal of the body really breaks down when we confront it by the admitted facts of the after-situation. For if the Priests induced Pilate to change the burial-place, or to authorize their doing so, they must have known the ultimate and final resting-place, and in that event they would never have been content with the obviously unsatisfactory and untrue statement that the disciples had stolen the body. They would surely have taken the much stronger ground that the body had been removed for judicial reasons by Pilate's command or at their own request. Such a statement, made on the authority of the High Priest, would have been final. It would have destroyed for ever the possibility of anyone credibly asserting the physical resurrection of Jesus, because in the last resort, and if challenged, the remains could always have been produced. It is the complete failure of anyone to produce the remains, or to point to any tomb, official or otherwise, in which they were said to lie, which ultimately destroys every theory based upon the human removal of the body.

4. *That Jesus did not really die on the Cross*

I include this suggestion here more for the sake of completeness than in the expectation that the reader will desire to hear it seriously argued. It is really little more than an historical curiosity. Driven by the immense strength and cogency of the case for the empty tomb, the German rationalist Venturini put forward the suggestion that Christ did not actually die upon the Cross, but fainted, and that in the cool temperature of the grave He recovered and subsequently appeared to the disciples.

This suggestion, while attempting to produce a strictly rational explanation of the post-Crucifixion phenomena, is surely the least rational of all. It ignores the deadly character of the wounds inflicted upon Jesus, the frightful laceration of the hands and feet, the loss of strength through the ebbing away of blood, the hopelessness of human aid during the critical moments when it would be most needed, the tight-drawn bandages of the grave, the heavy stone. To try even to think of what would happen to an utterly collapsed constitution, bleeding from five torn and untended wounds, lying on the cold slab of a tomb in April without human succour of any kind, is to realize at once the unreason of the argument. But the death-blow to this theory was dealt long ago by the distinguished critic, Strauss, in a passage which will repay study.[1]

---

[1] 'It is impossible that a being who had stolen half-dead out of the sepulchre, who crept about weak and ill, wanting medical treatment, who required bandaging, strengthening, and indulgence, and who still at last yielded to his sufferings, could have given to the disciples the impression that he was a conqueror over death and the grave, the Prince of Life: an impression which lay at the bottom of their future ministry. Such a resuscitation could only have weakened the impression which he had made upon them in life and in death, at the most could only have given it an elegiac voice, but could by no possibility have changed their sorrow into enthusiasm, have elevated their reverence into worship.' Strauss, *New Life of Jesus*, i, 412 (tr.).

5. *That the Women made a Mistake*

This brings us to a suggestion which can only be discussed fully when we have studied in some detail the historic encounter at the tomb, but there are certain broad and general consequences of the theory which can more conveniently be considered here.

The suggestion is that when Mary Magdalene and her friends came to the Garden on Sunday morning the light was very dim; indeed, that dawn was only just breaking. Things take unusual shapes in the semi-darkness, and it is thought that in these circumstances the women may have made a quite genuine mistake in identifying the grave. It is suggested that, on reaching a tomb which they unexpectedly found to be open they encountered a young man—the gardener has been indicated—who, recognizing their mission, tried to tell them that Jesus was not there. The women were terrified, however, at the discovery of their errand, and without waiting for the young man to finish his sentence and thus explain their mistake, they fled from the Garden.

It will be observed that this theory, despite its appearance of rationality, has one peculiar weakness. If it was so dark that the women accidentally went to the wrong tomb, it is exceedingly improbable that the gardener would have been at work. If it was late enough and light enough for the gardener to be at work, it is improbable that the women would have been mistaken. The theory thus rests upon the synchronization of two very doubtful contingencies. This is, however, only part of the improbability and intellectual difficulty which gathers around it.

In order that we may get this matter in the clearest possible light, I propose to take the statement of one of the ablest of its exponents, Prof. Kirsopp Lake, D.D., who has developed the theory with great fullness and lucidity in his book *The Resurrection of Jesus Christ*. I shall endeavour to give Dr. Lake's view as far as is possible in his own words, because the openness and candour of his style calls for an equal frankness in those who may be opposed to him. This is no place for mere dialectics. It is the theory itself that we want to study and understand.

Now Prof. Lake begins, and I think rightly, with the assumption that the story of the women's visit to the tomb is an authentic piece of history. Whatever view we may take of what happened later, this particular episode is embedded too deeply in the primitive literature to be treated other than with respect. The story of the women's adventure is in the earliest authentic document we possess, the Gospel of St. Mark. It is repeated by St. Matthew and St. Luke, it is confirmed so far as Mary Magdalene herself is concerned by St. John, it is in the Apocryphal Gospel of Peter; and, perhaps even more significantly, it is in that very ancient independent fragment, preserved by St. Luke in chapter xxiv., verses 13–24, the journey to Emmaus.

The essential historicity of the women's visit is, therefore, not at present in doubt. But Prof. Lake is inclined to question whether the tomb to which they came really was the original and authentic grave of Christ.

There are two main passages in which Prof. Lake develops his theme. In his chapter on 'The Facts behind the Tradition', he says:

'It is seriously a matter for doubt whether the women were really in a position to be quite certain that the tomb which they visited was that in which they had seen Joseph of Arimathea bury the Lord's body. . . . If it were not the same, the circumstances all seem to fall into line. The women came in the early morning to a tomb which they thought was the one in which they had seen the Lord buried. They expected to find a closed tomb, but they found an open one; and a young man, who was in the entrance, guessing their errand, tried to tell them that they had made a mistake in the place. "He is not here," said he; "see the place where they laid him", and probably pointed to the next tomb. But the women were frightened at the detection of their errand and fled, only imperfectly or not at all understanding what they heard. It was only later on, when they knew that the Lord was risen, and—on their view—that his tomb must be empty, that they came to believe that the young man was something more than they had seen; that he was not telling them of their mistake, but announcing the Resurrection, and that his intention was to give them a message for the disciples.'

The same idea is developed further in the following passage from 'The Narrative in Mark':

'The burial was watched, probably from a distance, by the little band of women who had remained to see the last moments of their Master. None of the other disciples were present, for they had scattered after the arrest of Jesus (St. Peter had a little later than the rest), and had either already returned home or were in hiding in Jerusalem until they could find an opportunity of escape.

'Soon all the disciples found themselves once more in their old home, and prepared to return to their old methods of life. But to their surprise the Lord appeared, first to St. Peter and afterwards to others—to those who lived in Judea as well as to the Galileans—and under the influence of these appearances of which the details have not been accurately preserved, they came to believe that the Lord was risen and exalted to Heaven, and that they were called to return to Jerusalem to take up their Master's work.

'In Jerusalem they found the women who had watched the burial, and these told them that they had gone on the morning of the third day to supply the deficiencies of the burial given to the Lord by Joseph, but when they came to the grave, instead of finding it closed, they found it open, and a young man terrified them by telling them that Jesus whom they were seeking was not there. Thus to the already firm belief in the fact of the Resurrection—a belief which to that generation implied that the grave was empty—came to be added, on the strength of the women's report, that the Resurrection took place on the third day.'

I have given these particular extracts because they seem to me to present, very clearly and in Prof. Lake's own words, the fundamentals of his case, viz.:

1. That the women probably made a mistake.
2. That they did not immediately report their discovery, because the disciples were no longer in Jerusalem.
3. That the latter only heard the story when they returned from Galilee after an interval of some weeks.

I do not propose to attempt here an examination of those subtler points in the original narratives which can only be studied effectively in the light of the far closer and more detailed investigation which we shall make in a later chapter. But there are three broad considerations which stand out and call for emphasis.

In the first place, the evidence for the supposed absence or inaccessibility of the disciples on Easter Sunday (so vital to Prof. Lake's interpretation of the case) seems to me to be of a very doubtful and precarious character. It rests solely upon a broken or partly completed sentence in St. Mark. Against this there is positive evidence of a most direct and demonstrative kind. Not only does St. Mark himself expressly imply the presence of the disciples[1] but the whole Synoptic tradition asserts and implies it too.

If there is one thing in the Gospel story which does not seem to admit of doubt it is that, although the earliest account says that the disciples forsook Jesus and fled, they did not *all* flee. One man among them at least braved the terrors of the city that night and even obtained access to the scene of the midnight trial. That man was Peter.

I do not know how the reader feels about this matter, but personally I am surer of the essential historicity of the pathetic little story of Peter's fall and repentance than of almost anything else in the Gospels. It is one of those stories which is intelligible enough as a transcript from real life, but which would be quite inexplicable regarded as fiction. What possible explanation can we offer of a story so damning and derogatory to the repute of one of the leading apostles getting into the first Christian account of the Passion save that it was an ineffaceable memory of an actual event.

If, therefore, Peter was manifestly present in Jerusalem on Friday morning, who can say with any confidence that he and his companions had fled the city by the following Sunday?

Secondly, the behaviour of the women themselves, according to this hypothesis, is so curiously unnatural and strange. Remember who these women are. We are not dealing with mere acquaintances of the apostolic band, but with their own kith and kin. Salome was the mother of two of the disciples; Mary of Cleophas, her sister, of two others.

---

[1] 'But go, tell his disciples and Peter, He goeth before you into Galilee: there shall ye see him, as he said unto you.'—Mark xvi. 7.

Moreover, they were not normally resident in the city; they had come up specially for the Feast. If the disciples as a body were in any pressing kind of danger, their women-folk were in like peril. They could not leave them indifferently to the machinations of the Priests or the fury of a section of the multitude. Some attempt to secure their safety and their speedy withdrawal from the city would assuredly be made.

This interdependence of the women upon the men very seriously embarrasses Prof. Lake's theory at its most vital point. Prof. Lake is compelled to keep the women in Jerusalem until Sunday morning, because he firmly believes that they really went to the tomb. He is also compelled to get the disciples out of Jerusalem before sunrise on Sunday because he holds that the women kept silence. Finally, to harmonize this with the fact that they did subsequently tell the story, with all its inevitable and logical results, he finds it necessary to keep the women in Jerusalem for several weeks while the disciples returned to their homes, had certain experiences, and came back to the capital.

What does Prof. Lake imagine these women were doing all these weeks, in a foreign town, with every instinct and domestic tie pulling them northward? Would he himself in similar circumstances have gone off to safety leaving his wife or his mother in a situation of unquestioned peril? I find it hard to believe. If it was safe for the women to remain in the city and go unostentatiously to the tomb of Jesus, it was safe for the disciples to remain also. If it was not safe for the disciples to remain, then Salome, Mary of Cleophas, and surely the stricken Mother of Jesus would have shared their flight.

But there is a far deeper and more radical difficulty than this. Neither Prof. Lake nor the Rev. P. Gardner-Smith, who has adopted the same view with slight reservations, seem to have realized the annihilating character of the evidential case which their theory, if true, would have placed within reach of the Priests. Caiaphas and his friends must have been very different men from what we take them for if they did not see instantly that the supreme answer to all this nonsense about an empty grave was *to produce the gardener*.

Here was the one man who could have spoken with complete and final authority; whose slightest word could have blown the whole flimsy story to the winds. Where are the traces of the controversy which must surely have followed so direct and damaging an appeal to the facts? Where is the confident statement of the Priests that the grave of Jesus was not vacant, and that the mouldering remains still lay within it? There is no trace of any such controversy or statement—only the faint echo of the original charge that the disciples themselves had abducted the body.

There are, indeed, two very good reasons why, as a matter of historic fact, this young man was never called as a witness by the enemies of Christianity. In the first place, as we shall see, he was probably not the gardener at all, and his presence at the cave in the dim light of Sunday morning was due to other causes. But the supreme and decisive factor lay in the fact that, throughout the early decades of Christianity, the physical vacancy of the authentic tomb of Christ was not in doubt. Events seem to have conspired to place that beyond the reach of argument.

6. *That the Grave was not visited by the Women*

This brings us to a theory which is, perhaps, the only really logical alternative to the Gospel thesis.

If it could be proved that that grave was not visited on Sunday morning, and that it lay undisturbed and perhaps unthought of for many months afterwards, then the rock upon which all the preceding hypotheses ultimately founder would be removed. For if the women did not announce its vacancy, the Priests would be under no compulsion to formulate a theory, and the city would have gone about its normal life, save for the inevitable excitement and discussion occasioned by so resounding an event as the Crucifixion.

Yet I submit that none of the six hypotheses which we have been considering falls in greater or completer intellectual ruin than this. As the sequel will show, the history of what happened afterwards belies it at every turn and corner of the road.

Chapter IX

THE HISTORIC CRUX OF THE PROBLEM

Whoever comes to this problem has sooner or later to confront a fact which cannot be explained away or removed by any logical processes whatsoever. It looks us persistently in the face as the one concrete and unassailably attested certainty of the situation.

This fact is that, some time between the close of the thirty-six hour gap and a period which we cannot reasonably place more than six or seven weeks later, a profound conviction came to the little group of people whose behaviour we have been considering that Jesus had risen from the grave.

The actual position is peculiar, and, I believe, quite unique in history. It is not that one or two emotional women who had been specially identified with the closing scenes of the Crucifixion received a presentiment that Jesus had risen and persistently asserted it in the teeth of hostile denials and the half-expressed doubts of their friends. Such a view of the situation will not stand a small part of the historic strain which has to be placed upon it. It is that *the whole party*, including the nine men who fled at the arrest, and certain independent persons who have not previously come into the story, were convinced that something had occurred which changed their entire outlook. It turned their dejection into triumph and their sorrow into an intense joy.

If the sole evidence for this really extraordinary phenomenon lay in a single passage in the early chapters of the Acts it would be possible to regard it as the rather exuberant record of a contemporary historian whose close connection with the movement had biased and coloured his views. But this is precisely what no one can claim. There is a far earlier and more authoritative testimony in the letters of Paul, of

103

Peter, of James the Just, and the admittedly historic network of Christian Churches stretching from Jerusalem through Asia Minor to the catacombs at Rome. Only from an intensely heated centre of burning zeal could this vast field of lava have been thrown out from a tiny country like Palestine to the limits of the Roman world. We cannot insist upon the strict reign of causality in the physical world, and deny it in the psychological. The phenomenon which here confronts us is one of the biggest dislodgments of events in the world's history, and it can only really be accounted for by an initial impact of colossal drive and power.

Yet the original material from which we have to derive this dynamic force consists of an habitual doubter like Thomas, a rather weak fisherman like Peter, a gentle dreamer like John, a practical tax-gatherer like Matthew, a few seafaring men like Andrew and Nathanael, the inevitable women, and at most two or three others.

I do not want to minimize the character of the historic nucleus from which Christianity sprang, but, seriously, does this rather heterogeneous body of simple folk, reeling under the shock of the Crucifixion, the utter degradation and death of their leader, look like the driving force we require? Frankly it does not, and the more we think of it disintegrating under the crisis the less can we imagine it rewelding into that molten focus which achieved those results. *Yet the clear evidence of history is that it did.* Something came into the lives of these very simple and ordinary people which transformed them out of all similitude to the broken and shattered party of Jesus which we have recently been studying.

What that experience was—whether it was physical, psychological, or both, or some transcendent happening outside the sphere of our immediate knowledge—is the real crux of our present study.

Before we proceed to a fuller and more detailed discussion of this question, however, there is one point which calls for special notice. According to the official history of these events—a document which was not only universally accepted from early times, but which comes from the pen of a writer who had exceptional facilities for learning what really did happen, the first public statement concerning the Resurrection of Jesus was made in Jerusalem during the Feast of Weeks—that is to say, the Feast immediately following the fatal Passover, and seven weeks after the date of the Crucifixion.

Why, in the first instance, this seven weeks' gap? It is a very pertinent and suggestive question. The date when the Acts was first committed to writing by St. Luke was at least some thirty or forty years after the events in question. There was time for the legend of the Resurrection—if legend it was—to have assumed its fullest and most developed form. Many of the actual eyewitnesses had passed away and a broad gulf of years lay between those who remained and the events themselves. The story which they would tell in A.D. 65 would either be the literal truth, which of course would be unassailable, or such a development of it as would carry the maximum conviction to the contemporary mind. The story would not tend to become *less convincing* as time went on. It would tend rather to lose its weak and incongruous elements, to shake out its awkward and inconvenient features.

Viewed, however, from the standpoint of pure legend this seven weeks' gap is an inconvenient feature, an anachronism of the first order. It does not help the credibility of the apostles' story. It embarrasses it. It provides an unnecessary and even incomprehensible stumbling-block to faith. It leaves the door wide open for the entry of the gravest suspicion. People would say: If Jesus rose from the dead on Easter Sunday and appeared to His disciples, why did they not proclaim it from the housetops at once? Why wait for seven weeks, until people had begun to forget about the great tragedy, and then suddenly spring their announcement upon the world?

It is difficult to conceive of a version of so momentous an occurrence as the Resurrection which would contain in itself so prolific a seed of doubt. If the story was a complete fiction it does small credit to its originators. Can we doubt that an absolutely untrammelled legend, told and retold many years after the event, would have avoided altogether so fatal a source of weakness and have placed the triumphant public announcement of the Resurrection on the very day that its discovery was made?

How then are we to regard this curious gap of seven weeks between the event itself and its first public affirmation? To my mind there can be only one satisfactory answer, viz. that we are here dealing, not with legend or romance, but with fact. The romancer can mould his incidents to fit his purpose, the biographer must take what life gives him.

I suppose that most of my readers have stood at some time or other upon some ancient road—a road that has served the needs of mankind for several centuries—and wondered why at a particular point it makes a sudden turn or detour to avoid, as it appears, *nothing*. There does not seem to be any reason why it should not have gone straight to its objective. The detour does not shorten the distance; it lengthens it. It does not make the gradient easier; very often it stiffens it. Why this incomprehensible loop or bend, when it would have been so much easier to have gone straight forward?

Whenever a situation like that occurs, if you will go back far enough into the history of that countryside, you will find the explanation in some vanished landmark, some enclosed space, or some established right which the common people, who made the road, could not dispute. The road bends and twists because there was something very real to be avoided.

It seems to me that something closely analogous occurs in the problem we are now studying. It would have been quite easy many years after the event, when Jerusalem lay in ruins and the sacred sites themselves were utterly lost in the debris of the final convulsion, to have invented a story of the Resurrection in which this strange element of the seven weeks' delay was entirely absent. Given the initial acceptance of the fact of the Resurrection at all, it would have sounded far more convincing to foreign ears if the announcement had followed forthwith upon the discovery. At that time there would have been no one effectively to dispute it. It would have seemed the necessary and logical result of so remarkable and outstanding an event.

But we are forgetting the people who originally made the road. The story of the Resurrection which was taught and preached throughout the ancient world during the first forty years of the Christian era was not told or created by outsiders, but by the original band of followers of Jesus. They did not wait two or three decades before giving their version to the world. They began their organized campaign within two months of the occurrences. Within three decades most of them had perished violently for their adhesion to this very story.

It is clear, therefore, that from the beginning the seven weeks' gap, with all its disconcerting loopholes and opportunities for the sceptic, was an integral part of the Christians' account of what happened. They told the story of those seven weeks, because it was the only story that truthful people could tell. It was the way things fell out. In other words, it was a fact of history.

Directly we realize this we begin to see that the supremely vital date when the great Christian declaration was first made publicly in Jerusalem cannot have been other than that of the Feast of Weeks in the Crucifixion year—the date which the Acts assigns to it; and the only date which Christian tradition has ever associated with it.

Consider now the manner in which this momentous declaration is reported to have been made. Jerusalem was passing through one of its periodic phases of high emotional activity. Again it was Feast time, and although there was probably not quite the same congestion as prevailed during the Passover, the city was full of visitors and pilgrims. With so many people present having no other object or occupation than the observance of the Feast, the narrow streets and bazaars of old Jerusalem were invariably animated and religious feeling ran high.

Now according to the Acts it was during this period that the event which we are considering took place, and the details which have been transmitted to us bear very strongly the impress of truth. We have to imagine a party of twelve or fourteen men and possibly some half-dozen women, suddenly emerging from a private dwelling-house in Jerusalem in a state of great emotional excitement. We have to think of a crowd quickly gathering about them; some openly scoffing and accusing the central group of over-indulgence in wine; others anxious to hear what the excitement was about. And we have to think of the fisherman Peter standing upon some eminence, possibly the steps of the house, and making a public explanation.

Obviously in some such way as this was the first public declaration of Christian experience made. But mark now the probable course of events. So long as the belief that Jesus had risen was nursed in private, declared and recounted only to intimates behind closed doors, the external situation in Jerusalem might have remained unchanged, but the moment the claim of the disciples was seriously and publicly circulated, it is obvious that two things were inevitable.

In the first place a heated controversy was unavoidable between the partisans of the new movement and those who were opposed to it. This was no ordinary difference of opinion upon a religious question of minor importance. It amounted to a great public scandal. If what the disciples said was true, then the priestly group which had pressed through and achieved the destruction of Jesus had betrayed the people and been guilty of the most heinous offence before God. If it was not true—if the whole thing was a pretence and a sham—then on moral grounds alone it ought to be exploded and stamped out at once. There was no possibility of taking up a half-way position. A man was either in favour of the new movement or very violently against it.

Secondly, however anxious the authorities might be to let the dangerous question of their policy against Jesus sleep, they could not ignore a campaign to preach their moral guilt under their very noses, and in the Temple precincts. Events would be too strong for them. They would be compelled into some repressive action in self-defence. To have failed to have done so would have been to abrogate their position, and to concur by silence.

It is clear from the testimony of the Acts that during the

four years when the Christian community was growing by leaps and bounds prior to the first great persecution under Saul of Tarsus, both these conditions were fulfilled. The leading apostles were arrested at least once, and possibly twice. The first occasion was ostensibly in connection with some trouble about a crippled man, but mainly and obviously owing to their teaching about Jesus. This is clearly shown by the fact that, on being released, they were adjured 'not to preach in that name' any more. It was the first fruitless attempt of authority to grasp the nettle which was destined to overrun and destroy the garden of its peace.

But side by side with this somewhat indecisive action on the part of the Jewish rulers—and perhaps explaining it—is the undisputable fact that Christianity was gaining adherents at a prodigious pace. The movement was spreading beyond all reasonable expectation. It does not seem to me seriously to matter whether the reader is prepared to take St. Luke's statement literally that three thousand people embraced the new faith on the first day or not. The terrific persecution of Saul, involving an inquisition to places as far distant as Damascus, shows that four years later it had grown to really alarming proportions. If the community which Saul tried to break up numbered no more than three thousand souls, it meant that three persons had been converted every day (including Sabbaths) for four years. This is a surprising rate of growth for so revolutionary a doctrine within the confines of Jerusalem itself, and the figure of three thousand souls is almost certainly underestimated.

Now the question which the reader will have to consider very seriously is whether it was possible for all this widespread agitation and conflict of ideas—involving as it did the definite claim that Jesus had risen—to have been conducted successfully, or indeed at all, in the actual and physical presence of the remains of Jesus. This is a concrete point to which we shall have repeatedly to return, for it is vital and quite fundamental to our understanding of the case.

Primarily, of course, it is a question of the evidence, and it is a noteworthy fact that such indications as we have point decisively in the opposite direction. Consider, first, a circumstance which has already been briefly alluded to in a previous chapter, but which now forces itself into special prominence. I mean the absence of any sign that the tomb of Jesus became an object of interest to His contemporaries, during the critical weeks and years which followed the Crucifixion.

It is impossible to read the records of the period without being profoundly impressed by the way in which, for friend and foe alike, the tomb of Jesus sinks into utter and undisturbed oblivion. No one in later years seems to have gone to Joseph's garden, and looking at the rock-hewn cave, to have said: 'This is the place where the Lord is buried.' No hostile investigation seems to have been made to show that the martyred remains of the great Teacher still lay where they were deposited some days, weeks, or months earlier. Still more strikingly, no one pretending to have an intimate and special knowledge seems to have said: 'Not here was He ultimately buried, but there.' Instead of these quite natural consequences flowing from so extraordinary an event, we get this stony appearance of indifference. From the moment that the women return from the Garden, the tomb of Jesus passes, historically, into complete oblivion.

Now this is really extraordinary. Whichever way we look at it, it is a very formidable fact, and it challenges examination. After all, the number of people in Jerusalem who were intimately known to Jesus during His lifetime and who might be subject to some kind of illusion upon the occasion of His death was really quite small and inconsiderable. If we reckon them at thirty we shall probably be well within the mark. This minute body was scattered among a vast concourse of pilgrims from the provinces and distant countries, numbering in all some hundreds of thousands. One would have thought that out of this great and varied multitude there would have been not a few to whom the decisive issue was the condition of the grave, that a controversy would have sprung up as to its contents; and that the issue would have been hotly disputed on both sides.

But there is no trace of any such controversy. The assumption that the tomb was empty seems to have been universal.

The only controversy of which we have any record, and it was clearly a heated one, was on the vexed question as to whether the disciples had secretly removed the body. This, I say, is a very formidable fact. It suggests that something had already occurred to make the vacancy of the tomb common ground, and to place it high out of the reach of dispute or argument.

*　　*　　*　　*　　*

But it is not only the oblivion of the tomb which is so arresting. There is the curious and opposite fact that its vacancy cannot be denied without creating an intolerable position from the reasoned and logical point of view.

Consider the position in Jerusalem a few weeks from the extreme radical and negative standpoint. The party of Jesus has returned to the capital after an uncertain period of sojourn in distant Galilee. It may have been three weeks or it may have been six or seven. The precise length of the gap is immaterial, for in either case the intense passions engendered by the Crucifixion would have tended to die down. During the period of their absence the individual members of the party have undergone an experience which has changed their whole outlook. Dwelling continuously upon the events of the past two years, and especially upon certain obscure sayings of Jesus which were not understood at the time, they have become convinced that Jesus has risen and has been 'exalted', as they put it, 'to the right hand of God'. This belief has been greatly intensified by certain experiences on the part of one or more members of the party who are convinced that the risen Jesus has appeared to them with the marks of His passion in His flesh. These experiences are communicated to the others who are already in the mood to believe, and in due course the whole party, the men as well as the women, set out for Jerusalem to proclaim the truth that Jesus was, therefore, in very truth the Messiah.

(I have tried to present the radical case with fairness and justice. If the reader feels that, stated thus, it lacks conviction, let him try to strengthen it. He will find how extraordinarily difficult it is to put the case more vigorously with due regard to psychological probability.)

Now it is hardly possible to make a greater mistake than to assume that when we have accounted for the conversion of the disciples we have accounted also for the sudden and very rapid rise of Christianity. The crucial test has to come.

We have to bring these convinced but (according to the hypothesis) really deluded people into the very heart of the city where the awkward and irremovable tomb lies, where people have been going about their work daily for weeks believing that the grave has never been interfered with, and who have now come to accept the official coup philosophically as representing ultimately the will and purpose of God. And we have to think of them as setting out to convert this great and varied community to their own view and belief.

Primarily and outstandingly this stupendous attempt at evangelization had, necessarily, to take the form of an appeal, not to the emotions, but to the intellect. The Jews were a very logical people, and we have only to read the address of Stephen, the speech of Paul from the fortress steps, and the other preserved utterances in the Acts to see how invariably the Christian leaders sought to appeal to the minds and judgments of their hearers. As we shall see later, the controversy engendered by the declaration of the disciples was a fierce intellectual controversy which raged for many months in every synagogue where the pretensions of the Christians were seriously raised.

If we could imagine all this taking place in Capernaum or Tiberias, or any town far remote from the scene of the trial and Crucifixion, it would be possible to think of it as meeting with some measure of success. A really convinced body of people on the one hand, with no ready means of testing or obtaining exact data, might have led to numerous converts, though whether the Church could have held them is another matter.

But history decrees that this controversy had to be fought out in *Jerusalem* where no real illusions could prevail, where anybody could go and see the tomb between supper and bed-time, and where an overwhelming body of official, authoritative and conclusive witness existed. Yet it is in this centre of solid and conservative realism that, according to St. Luke, no fewer than three thousand converts were made in one day, increased shortly afterwards to five thousand.

What was the determining factor in this steady erosion into the Judean body which in a few short years became so serious and widespread that Saul of Tarsus was driven to organize a tremendous campaign of suppression against it? Whence came the drive which convinced one reasonable person after another that the Christians were right and the Priests were in the wrong? Could anything have prospered with the disciples if in addition to the denials of the Priests, and the real doubts and waverings of the populace, the tomb itself had given a silent and impenetrable No!?

But there is another aspect of this question which must not be overlooked. I mean how it was that the disciples themselves came to believe in this astonishing thing.

We have been proceeding rather on the assumption that we can postulate anything of the disciples providing that it accounts, superficially at least, for their behaviour. But to the student who makes the human mind his province there is no knottier or more baffling problem than this. We know these eleven men better than we know any other single group of persons in antiquity. Their characters are written plainly in the narratives, and Jesus Himself who chose them was no mean judge of mental and spiritual qualities.

In the early stages of our reconstruction we rejected the suggestion that the disciples stole the body of Jesus on the ground that it was repugnant and exclusive to their known moral qualities and to their singularly unimaginative type of mind. But difficulties not less insuperable present themselves when we try to think of them uniformly and without exception coming under the influence of a complete delusion. Somehow the rugged fisherman Peter and his brother Andrew, the characteristically doubting Thomas, the seasoned and not too sensitive tax-gatherer, Matthew, the rather dull Philip, intensely loyal but a little slow of apprehension, do not fit easily into the conditions required for an absolutely unshakable collective hallucination. And if it is not both collective and unshakable it is of no use to us. The terrors and the persecutions which these men ultimately had to face and did face unflinchingly, do not admit of a half-hearted adhesion secretly honeycombed with doubt. The belief has to be unconditional and of adamantine strength to satisfy the conditions. Sooner or later, too, if the belief was to spread it had to bite its way into the corporate consciousness by convincing argument and attempted proof.

Now the peculiar thing about this phenomenon is that, not only did it spread to every single member of the Party of Jesus of whom we have any trace, but they brought it to Jerusalem and carried it with inconceivable audacity into the most keenly intellectual centre of Judea, against the ablest dialecticians of the day, and in the face of every impediment which a brilliant and highly organized camarilla could devise. *And they won.* Within twenty years the claim of these Galilean peasants had disrupted the Jewish Church and impressed itself upon every town on the Eastern littoral of the Mediterranean from Cæsarea to Troas. In less than fifty years it had begun to threaten the peace of the Roman Empire.

When we have said everything which can be said about the willingness of certain types of people to believe what they want to believe, to be carried away by their emotions, and to assert as fact what has originally reached them as hearsay, we stand confronted with the greatest mystery of all. *Why did it win?*

The Christian Church drew its steadily mounting numbers not from the occasional visitors to the Feasts, but from the resident population of Jerusalem. We have to account not merely for the enthusiasm of its friends, but for the paralysis of its enemies and for the ever-growing stream of new converts which came over to it. When we remember what certain highly placed personages in Jerusalem would almost certainly have given to have strangled this movement at its birth but could not—how one desperate expedient after another was adopted to silence the apostles, until that veritable bow of Ulysses, the Great Persecution, was tried and broke in pieces in their hands—we begin to realize that behind all these subterfuges and makeshifts there must have stood a silent, unanswerable fact, a fact which geography and the very fates themselves had made immovable. We realize also why it was that throughout the four years when Christianity was growing to really formidable dimensions in Jerusalem, neither Caiaphas, nor Annas, nor any recognized member of the Sadducean camarilla, whose prestige and personal repute was so deeply affronted and outraged by the new doctrine, ever took the obvious short cut out of their difficulties.

If the body of Jesus still lay in the tomb where Joseph had deposited it, why did they not say so? A cold and dispassionate statement of the real facts, issued by someone in authority, and publicly exhibited in the Temple precincts, would have been like a douche of water upon the kindling fire of the Christian heresy. It would have steadied the situation in their favour. It would have impeded immensely, if not destroyed, the growing daily stream of new converts.

Apparently they did nothing of the kind, for the reason that they could not. In all the fragments and echoes of this far-off controversy which have come down to us we are nowhere told that any responsible person asserted that the body of Jesus was still in the tomb. We are only given reasons why it was not there. Running all through these ancient documents is the persistent assumption that the tomb of Christ was vacant.

Can we fly in the face of this cumulative and mutually corroborative evidence? Personally, I do not think we can. The sequence of coincidences is too strong. When we remember the swinging round of the disciples from panic fear to absolute certitude, the singular matter of the seven weeks' gap, the extraordinarily rapid adhesion of converts in Jerusalem, the strange absence of administrative vigour on the part of the authorities, the steady growing of the Church, both in authority and power, until the whole situation blew up into the frenzied attempts at suppression under Saul, we realize that we are in the presence of something far more tangible than the psychological repercussion of a fisherman's dream.

The vacant tomb itself must have been the final and unanswerable objective witness. It could not be got rid of by either side. By the very irony of fate the disciples were committed to prosecuting their campaign within a quarter of an hour's walk of the place in which, if their contention was false, the mouldering remains of their great Leader lay. The practical issue could be settled at first hand, immediately, and by any number of witnesses. If the women's statement was true, and the remains of Jesus were no longer in the tomb, it would be as easy to test that fact as it was for the women to make the original discovery seven weeks earlier. Even Joseph would not permanently seal an empty chamber intended for his own use.

Thus by another converging line of thought we come back to the point from which we started. However baffling and disconcerting it may seem at first sight, the evidence for the essential accuracy of the women's story is overwhelming in its consistency and strength. It is the kind of evidence which impresses by its quiet unobtrusiveness, its steady pointing in one direction. Yet, as we shall see, the direction remains unchanged when we test the same historic situation by another and a greater criterion, the personal witness of certain people whose right to be heard is absolute and whose authority cannot be gainsaid.

Chapter X

THE EVIDENCE OF THE PRINCIPAL
FISHERMAN

There are three men in particular whose testimony concerning this matter, if it could be obtained, would be
absolutely final and conclusive. The first is the fisherman, Peter, who himself led the attack upon Jerusalem,
and who was for several years the unchallenged leader of the
movement. The second is the Prisoner's brother, James the
Just, who for some extraordinary reason threw in his lot
with the Christians and who ultimately perished for the
cause. The third is a certain man Saul, from Tarsus, who,
backed by the full power of the State, tried to smash the
movement and was eventually engulfed by it.

All these three men thus came under the spell of the post-
Crucifixion experiences of Christianity. They all suffered
the extreme penalty of their convictions after the manner of
that barbaric age—James in Jerusalem itself; Peter and Saul
in Rome. If we could learn what each of these outstanding
primary witnesses for Christianity believed and taught
about the Resurrection, many obscure points in our study
would be made clear. Let us consider first the case of Peter.

When the veil lifts, and the united party of Jesus is discovered in Jerusalem, the man we find in a position of unquestioned leadership and authority is not the man whom,
on purely psychological grounds, we might have been led to
expect. It is not the intimate friend of Jesus, and trusted
disciple, John. It is not the practical Matthew. It is not the
fervent idealist, Nathanael. It is a certain fisherman named
Simon, who later came to be called Peter.

Fortunately the earlier history of this rugged fisherman is
better known to us than that of any single member of the

party, and many of the facts recorded about him are of a kind which mere adulators would not have reported, still less have *invented*. They stick out from the narrative by their sheer awkwardness, their uncompromising fidelity to truth.

Take for example the severe rebuke which Jesus is reported to have addressed to him while they were wandering in the neighbourhood of Cæsarea Philippi: 'Get thee behind me Satan, for thou savourest not the things that be of God.' This is not the kind of reminiscence which would do a man's reputation any good, especially when it appeared in a quasi-official document read Sunday by Sunday in a large proportion of the Churches of Christendom. There can be only one intelligible reason for its inclusion and acceptance. It was an historic part of the whole gamut of strange experiences by the disciples during the great Ministry, and it had to remain.

Or take that other and even more famous episode, upon which the fierce light of publicity has beaten through all the centuries—the denial of Jesus by Peter in the outer Court of the High Priest's house. This episode belongs unmistakably to the historic recollections of those far-off days. What possible explanation can we devise of this humiliating story appearing in an admittedly pro-Christian document, bearing the name of the friend and interpreter of Peter, other than the perfectly natural and consistent one that it was the stark and naked truth. If evidence were needed of the high standard of veracity prevailing in the Early Church we have it here in its most convincing form.

If, therefore, we are compelled to accept these less heroic episodes in the life of Peter as a direct transcript from life, we are surely on firm historic ground when we take the softer details in the Gospel portraiture as depicting with great truth and fidelity the man himself. We find him on the whole a very lovable person, possessing possibly a rough exterior but an intensely warm and loyal heart; rather impulsive; quickly roused to sudden anger, but as quick to perceive and acknowledge the error of his ways. It is the glory of this type of man that he is peculiarly susceptible to reason when the hot rush of some sudden emotion is past.

Moreover, he was a fisherman by trade, with the Galilean peasant's ingrained simplicity of character. There is no trace in the Gospels of any special subtlety or intellectual brilliance. The dialectical dilemmas by which Christ occasionally turned the more deadly shafts of the Pharisees were probably less obvious to Peter than to some of his companions. He seems to have led, and to have been the spokesman of the party, partly on account of his seniority, but chiefly because of his sterling human worth. He was so transparently open, frank, and in earnest—so completely and unconsciously free from what, today, we should call 'side'. It was this man who, on behalf of the entire surviving body of original adherents, and with their obvious consent and concurrence, made the ringing claim that Jesus had risen from the grave. He is reported to have made it in Jerusalem within a few weeks of the Crucifixion, and with a certain decisiveness of language which calls for the closest study.

So far as St. Luke's testimony itself goes there can be of course no question as to the purport of Peter's teaching. The language attributed to him on the memorable occasion when he stood up and made the first historic declaration to the assembled crowd on the day of Pentecost is extraordinarily clear and definite. Moreover, there is a certain primitive quality about the phraseology of his speech which stamps it as belonging to a much earlier stratum of belief than that which prevailed when the historian actually wrote. The exact words are worth studying:

'Ye men of Judæa, and all ye that dwell at Jerusalem, be this known unto you, and give ear unto my words. For these are not drunken, as ye suppose; seeing it is but the third hour of the day. . . . Ye men of Israel, hear these words: Jesus of Nazareth, a man approved of God unto you by mighty works and wonders and signs, which God did by him in the midst of you, even as ye yourselves know; him, being delivered up by the determinate counsel and fore-knowledge of God, ye by the hand of lawless men did crucify and slay: whom God raised up, having loosed the pangs of death: because it was not possible that he should be holden of it. . . . This Jesus did God raise up, whereof we are all witnesses.'

Mark first the very significant words: '*Jesus of Nazareth, a man approved of God.*' Long before the time when the Acts was first written, the Christian community had ceased to speak of Jesus in this particular way. He had become an object of veneration, even of worship. Thus the very phraseology of the speech betrays an early and primitive source. It breathes the kind of atmosphere we should have expected within seven or eight weeks of the Crucifixion itself.

But when we come to the explicit references to the Resurrection we find an equally early and contemporary note.

'This Jesus did God raise up, whereof we all are witnesses.'

The phrase is direct and immediate. It fits something which has recently happened. It would be inappropriate to an event long past. Moreover, it is repeated in closely similar language on three separate occasions in the early chapters of Acts.

If, as some critics have suggested, these varied speeches are really independent accounts of the *same event*, then the similarity of the phrasing is very significant. It suggests that we have here a clearly remembered and actual transcript of Peter's speech. Versions which differ so widely in the details, but come abruptly to fundamental agreement concerning this one phrase, are very noteworthy as evidence.

Thus the testimony of the Acts, written of course many years after the event, is explicit that the fisherman, Peter, who was then the dominating figure of the movement, taught the Resurrection of Jesus in what, having regard to the context, can only be regarded as the full physical sense. In this he was apparently supported and upheld by the united party for which he spoke.

But there is really a much stronger and more convincing bit of evidence embedded in this ancient record than anything which Peter himself is reported to have said. It consists of something which, according to St. Luke, he did *not* say.

It will be remembered that according to Dr. Lake's theory of these events the women who went to the tomb in the early dawn of Sunday morning did not immediately report their discovery, because the disciples were supposed to be in hiding or to have fled already to Galilee. It was suggested that they remained in Jerusalem throughout the period when the rest of the party were undergoing their strange experience in Galilee, and that it was not until several weeks later, when the men returned in a body to Jerusalem, that the story of the women's adventure came out.

Everyone will surely agree that, even if the women did originally keep silence owing to the supposed absence or flight of the disciples, that silence must have been broken immediately the two parties came together again. We cannot reasonably imagine Peter and the entire Apostolic band returning to Jerusalem full of their conviction that they had seen Jesus without the women at once recounting their adventure at the grave. The two experiences were so absolutely complementary. Nay more, the women's testimony, coming as a new and hitherto unknown fact, would seem to be a crowning proof of the reality of their own experience. Not only would it strengthen their own conviction, but it would furnish a most powerful lever for the conversion of others. We should naturally expect Peter, therefore, to bring out prominently this surprising confirmation of the disciples' claim in the speech which he made from the steps of the house. He was announcing an almost incredible thing to an incredulous crowd. He was manifestly anxious to convert the people to his own belief. According to St. Luke these very women were probably standing in the little group surrounding Peter when he made the speech. Yet there is not a solitary word, either about them or their discovery. And in two subsequent speeches which he made, and which are reported quite fully in the Acts, the same startling omission is manifest.

It is possible, superficially at least, to explain this fact by saying that Peter did not know of the women's visit to the grave. If that were indeed true, then nothing would be more certain than that the women never went to the grave at all. If Mary of Cleophas and Salome and Joanna had not told their most intimate friends and kinsmen, after seven weeks' absence, of the most momentous and surprising episode of all that tragic week-end within ten minutes of their coming together, it was because there was nothing to tell, and all that strangely moving and human story was a palpable and utterly baseless invention of later days. Yet we may search the Acts through and through and we shall find no hint or whisper of this story of the women covertly emerging into view. No breath of any controversy arising from it is reflected even in the earliest of the Epistles. From the moment that these women make this last appearance upon the page of history they sink, like the vacated tomb itself, into undisturbed oblivion, save that the unforgettable memory of their adventure is embedded deeply in every document and every scrap of written recollection treasured by the Church.

How can we account for this strange silence going right back through the earliest Epistles to the very opening proclamation of the Faith on the day of Pentecost? There is one explanation which is big enough to stand four square to all the many-sided aspects of this very complex situation. It lies in the simple assumption that the Gospels are right, and that a secret so far-reaching in its consequences could not have remained locked for seven weeks in the bosoms of three or four women.

By nightfall on Easter Sunday the essential facts must have been known in Jerusalem, not only to those in high places, but as a quiver of rumour throughout the whole city. Men setting out to walk to a distant village that evening apparently knew sufficient of the details to declare that 'certain women of our company amazed us, having been early at the tomb'. Within twenty-four hours at most the story must have been public property. Explanation was met by counter-explanation, charge by counter-charge. And high above all these vulgar wranglings came the sinister suggestion: 'The disciples have stolen the body.'

If that be assumed we can understand why it was that seven weeks later when, upon the initiative of the disciples themselves, the whole question of the Resurrection was brought into the sharpest focus and lifted to the level of a great national and political controversy, no recognized

122

leader of the Christians thought it necessary to bring forward the evidence of the women.

The reason for this very significant silence seems to be clear. *The physical fact for which the women alone could vouch did not stand in need of any proof or argument.* It was notorious, and had been so already for seven weeks. If St. Paul's Cathedral were to be burned down this evening the fact that the policeman on point duty in Cheapside was the first to discover the outbreak would be a matter of some interest and would almost certainly appear in any subsequent history. But no one would dream, two months later, of calling the constable to prove that the great and historic edifice had been destroyed.

Indeed, if the historian of the future, delving into the faded volumes of *The Times*, found that seven weeks after the date usually given for the outbreak a prominent public man actually cited the policeman's testimony as evidence of the catastrophe it would create the gravest doubt as to the reality of the occurrence.

Thus, whether we consider the recorded speeches in the Acts or their even more significant omissions, we reach the conclusion that the witness of the fisherman Peter to the physical vacancy of the grave is beyond question. But we have still to consider another and an independent witness. For above and behind all this stands the massive and very impressive witness of St. Mark.

I agree profoundly with all that Dr. Lake has said in that carefully studied chapter about the primitive character and essential trustworthiness of St. Mark. Historically that document is unique. It stands like a great rock far out to sea, washed by the incoming tide long before the coastline of the distinctively Christian literature is reached. It casts its mighty shadow across all that littoral. It divides the very waters that flow towards it.

That this rugged and uncompromising old document stands in a special relationship to the teaching of Peter has been a tradition of the Church from the very dawn of Christendom and will be disputed by few. It has the simple directness of his frank and objective mind. It is markedly deficient in that smooth polish which a more literary and cultured pen could have given to it. It is singularly synoptic, abrupt, and reminiscent of disconnected utterances and recollections.

Jesus Himself once said: 'Search the scriptures, for these are they that testify of me.' So this rugged old fisherman might arise from his grave, as Mr. Chesterton has pictured the great heresiarchs arising, and say: 'Search Mark, for therein will you find the essence of my teaching.'

If this indeed be the case, then any real doubt as to what Peter himself taught and believed must be set at rest. For in the very heart of this primitive and ancient document which some have said contained a passage so outspoken and damaging to the Church that it was deliberately destroyed and lost for ever to the world, there stands that wonderful and arresting passage, pellucid in its clarity as a lunar landscape, yet cold and objective as the dawn:

'And when the sabbath was past, Mary Magdalene and Mary the mother of James, and Salome, bought spices, that they might come and anoint him. And very early on the first day of the week, they come to the tomb when the sun was risen.'

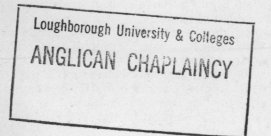

Chapter XI

THE EVIDENCE OF THE PRISONER'S BROTHER

With one single exception, which I shall deal with later, there is nothing in the whole of this strange story which impresses me so profoundly as the part played by the individual known to the ancient church as James, the Lord's brother, or, alternatively, as James the Just.

We are not entirely dependent for our knowledge of this man upon sources favourable to the Christian faith. Like Pilate and certain outstanding personalities of the early Christian era, he is mentioned by Josephus, a writer notoriously contemptuous of the whole movement. Moreover, some independent details are given by Hegesippus, the father of Church history, in some fragments preserved by Eusebius.

It will be convenient if we trace his record backwards, beginning with the famous paragraph in which Josephus describes his death. The passage from Josephus is as follows:

'Festus was now dead, and Albinus was but upon the road; so he (Ananus, the high priest) assembled the Sanhedrin of Judges and brought before them the brother of Jesus who was called Christ; whose name was James, and some others; and when he had formed an accusation against them as breakers of the law, he delivered them to be stoned.'

The year in which this occurred was A.D. 62, when events were driving hard towards that fatal insurrection which was to bring Titus and his armies to the walls of Jerusalem. The passage, brief as it is, tells us clearly two things. First, that James was widely known as the 'brother of Jesus'. Secondly, that he suffered martyrdom for his adhesion to the Cause. Thus the two most significant facts about him are guaranteed by no less an authority than Josephus himself.

The first date which attracts our attention as we glance backwards over the span of this man's life is approximately five years earlier, A.D. 57. Paul was visiting Jerusalem for what proved to be the last time. He had sailed with Luke and possibly certain others from Troas to Cæsarea, where he picked up Mnason, of Cyprus, and journeyed thence to the great city. St. Luke tells the story in Acts xxi with some fullness, for he was an eye-witness, and this is one of the 'we' sections. Then in the midst of the description comes this passage:

'And when we were come to Jerusalem, the brethren received us gladly. And the day following Paul went in with us unto James; and all the elders were present. And when he had saluted them, he rehearsed one by one the things which God had wrought among the Gentiles by his ministry.'

The phrase 'he went in unto James, and the elders were present' confirms what we know from other sources, viz. that at this particular time James was the dominant figure of the Christian Movement in Jerusalem. He had risen to become head of the resident mother church. His authority was far-reaching and paramount. It was to him, as representing Christianity at the very cradle of its inception, that Paul went to report upon his mission.

The impression thus obtained is confirmed and enriched by new details when we go back another seven years to A.D. 50. Here we get a far clearer picture of James than anywhere else. It was the occasion of the famous Council of Jerusalem, called to consider and decide upon the most momentous question of policy which the young movement had then been called upon to face. The campaign to the Gentiles, so energetically pursued by Paul and others, with Syrian Antioch as its headquarters, was making headway—tremendous headway in some directions—but the peculiarly Jewish rites imposed by the Mosaic Law, and especially the rite of circumcision, was a grievous stumbling-block to many foreign converts.

It was to remove this stumbling-block that a deputation consisting of Paul and Barnabas was sent from the Antiochean community to Jerusalem. They were received with every mark of affection and esteem, and after Peter had spoken in marked favour of the visitors' point of view, we find James giving what is clearly the casting and presidential vote.

'Brethren, hearken unto me: Symeon hath rehearsed how first God did visit the Gentiles, to take out of them a people for his name. And to this agree the words of the prophets. . . . Wherefore my judgment is, that we trouble not them which from among the Gentiles turn to God; but that we write unto them, that they abstain from the pollution of idols, and from fornication, and from what is strangled, and from blood. For Moses from generations of old hath in every city them that preach him, being read in the synagogues every sabbath. Then it seemed good to the apostles and the elders, with the whole church, to choose men out of their company, and send them to Antioch with Paul and Barnabas.'

It is necessary to go back another six years to A.D. 44 to read the next outstanding reference to James. It arose out of the second imprisonment of Peter. The young community was passing through dark and perilous days. Peter, as the chief spokesman of the party, was always in some personal danger, and for the second time he was apprehended and thrown into prison. By some means, widely attributed to supernatural intervention, he escaped or was released in the middle of the night. Apparently realizing that it would be perilous, both for himself and for his friends, to join them openly he made his way unobtrusively to the house of John Mark.

How, when Peter knocked, the inmates were too terrified to respond until the girl Rhoda recognized Peter's voice, is familiar to all readers of the Acts, but the significant sentence for our present purpose is in the message which Peter left before disappearing again into the night.

'Tell these things unto James, and to the brethren.'

Clearly James, in the absence of Peter himself, was the predominant figure and the leader-designate of the party.

There is still one earlier and very famous reference to James by name, this time in a quite independent document, the letter written by Paul from Antioch. The event to which it refers occurred in A.D. 36.

'Then after three years I went up to Jerusalem to visit Cephas, and tarried with him fifteen days. But other of the apostles saw I none, save James the Lord's brother.'

Thus as early as A.D. 36 this man James was a prominent figure in the early community, sharing with Peter (and as verse 9 shows, with John) the leadership of the party.

How did it come about this man, whose coldness and even hostility towards Christ during the living Ministry is written plainly in the earliest record—whose whole training and sympathies led him to incline towards the official and priestly view—is found in the inner circle and councils of the Christians? I ask that question not with any intent to score an empty point, but because the fact itself is so conspicuously challenging and amazing. One would have expected to find James anywhere but in the deluded circle of the Nazarenes.

It is understandable enough that St. Luke and the writers of the later Gospels, having the manifest fidelity of James before their eyes, should have softened down the many stories current of the earlier hostility of the brethren of Jesus. No well-disposed and friendly person willingly rakes up old scores when the wounds themselves are healing. But the primitive Gospel of St. Mark leaves us in no doubt that this hostility existed, and there are certain notable sayings among the recorded utterances of Christ which must have been occasioned by it.

The witness of St. Mark concerning this matter is very definite and circumstantial. It would seem that at the time when Jesus emerged from obscurity into the fierce light of His public ministry Joseph was already dead. We hear nothing of him whatever. It is the Mother of Jesus and 'his brethren' who periodically come into the picture. If there were a scintilla of evidence that any real bond of sympathy existed between these brothers and the revolutionary genius of Christ—if there were even an indication of that spirit of

128

hero-worship with which younger members of a family sometimes regard the outstanding gifts and achievements of a brilliant elder brother—we could understand in some measure what happened in later years.

But of this there is not a trace. Such evidence as exists is wholly and uncompromisingly against it. There are two passages in the third chapter of St. Mark which have to be read together if we are to get their meaning, for they are both part of one episode:

1. 'And he cometh into a house. And the multitude cometh together again, so that they could not so much as eat bread. And when his friends heard it, they went out to lay hold on him: for they said, He is beside himself.'

2. 'And there come his mother and his brethren; and, standing without, they sent unto him, calling him. And a multitude was sitting about him; and they say unto him, Behold, thy mother and thy brethren without seek for thee. And he answereth them, and saith, Who is my mother and my brethren?'

It seems obvious from a careful reading of this chapter that the 'friends' of Jesus referred to in the earlier quotation were His *relatives*, and that the whole object of their coming to the door of the house and calling was to get Him away. The explanation given is that in their view He was 'beside Himself' or, as we should put it to-day, that His mind was unhinged.

That this was the meaning of St. Mark is, I think clear, and the studied and even scornful disregard of their appeal by Christ endorses it.

'And looking round on them which sat round about him, he saith, Behold, my mother and my brethren! For whosoever shall do the will of God, the same is my brother, and sister, and mother.'

This, however, is not the only occasion when a marked coldness and antipathy between Jesus and His family comes out. Three chapters later St. Mark records what is purely an historic recollection of an uneffaceable incident in the personal life of Jesus. Sooner or later, in the course of His preaching tours in Galilee, He was bound to come to

Nazareth. When He came and preached in the village synagogue, He was openly discredited.

'And when the sabbath was come, he began to teach in the synagogue: and many hearing him were astonished, saying, Whence hath this man these things? and, What is the wisdom that is given unto this man, and what means such mighty works wrought by his hands? Is not this the carpenter, the son of Mary, the brother of James, and Joses, and Judas, and Simon? and are not his sisters here with us? And they were offended in him.'

The reply which Jesus then made has resounded since throughout the world:

'And Jesus said unto them, A prophet is not without honour, save in his own country, *and among his own kin*, and in his own house.'

The words which I have rendered in italics are peculiar. *They occur only in St. Mark.* Why did St. Matthew soften this passage by omitting these particular words altogether? Why did St. Luke go still further and omit the reference even to His own house? St. Luke especially has usually a reason for his literary emendations. Is not the most likely reason that the revered and deeply respected James was still alive or that his memory was too fresh to warrent a needless stab at his early unbelief?

How does all this strike you? What is it about the death of Jesus which brought such curiously dissimilar people into the narrow pathway which led to persecution, humiliation and often a tortured death? Why did so many normal yet diverse people, shortly after the great Tragedy, swing over and become utterly convinced that Jesus had risen from the grave?

It is easy to invent reasons why a man here or a woman there might have come under the spell of this extraordinary delusion. But the present case is different. In all this strange business of the culminative conversion of so many diverse and contrasted minds, there is a sense of something lurking in the background—some silent but unanswerable fact which brooked neither challenge nor mental doubt.

I have brought forward the case of this man James, not

because he is central or even necessary to the argument, but, in a sense, because he is not. The miracle of the conversion of the disciples would still remain a miracle, though no hint had survived concerning the attitude of James. He was outside the original circle of the apostles and their friends. He could have had few, if any, illusions concerning his own brother. He stood just sufficiently far apart to be an impartial witness, and yet so near to Christ that, had the Priests been able to command his allegiance, his influence alone might have changed the face of history. But they could not, and they slew him in the end.

It is said that the Christians inscribed upon his monument the words: 'He hath been a true witness both to Jews and Greeks that Jesus is Christ.' Having regard to who he was it might almost be said that his testimony is unique. It would have been unique had his experience not been eclipsed utterly by that other and even greater hostile witness, who came from Tarsus, and whose name was Saul.

Chapter XII

THE EVIDENCE OF THE MAN FROM TARSUS

It is almost impossible to imagine anything more fortunate from a purely historical point of view than the fact that, just at the moment when Christianity was taking the measure of its adversaries, there chanced to come to Jerusalem a young man, who, judged even by high modern standards, can claim to be a very competent and almost impartial observer.

The name of this young man was Saul. He was a Hebrew of very careful upbringing, intensely zealous in the performance of his religious duties, but with a mind broadened by contact with the wider life and speculative thinking of the Græco-Roman world. He was acquainted with some at least of the writings of Aratus, of Epimenides and of Menander, as his later speeches show. And he hailed from Tarsus, in Cilicia. The year was about A.D. 34.

The fact with which we have chiefly to deal in this chapter is that this young man, coming with some freshness to the problem, began by being the outstanding figure on one side of the controversy and ended in being the outstanding figure on the other. He attempted to suppress the movement by force, but was himself suppressed and assimilated by it.

Thus, to the long line of singular conversions—the conversion of Peter and Matthew and Philip; of the women Salome, Mary, and Joanna; of the hostile James; of Matthias of Barsabbas and the rest—we have to add that of this fresh and independent observer. As every serious student of the problem will agree, this is a phenomenon which cannot be evaded or side-tracked. It must be faced. We must learn what it was that first threw this young man Saul so vehemently on the side of the Priests, and what is involved by his complete intellectual transfer to the other side.

I propose, therefore, in the first instance, to examine with some care the situation which must have prevailed in Jerusalem at the time when Saul came upon the scene and for a short period afterwards.

*   *   *   *   *

It is clear that when Saul of Tarsus first came into prominence as a protagonist in this affair, a public controversy must have been going on for a considerable time. The movement had grown from its original nucleus of nineteen or twenty people to a large following requiring seven deacons to deal with and supervise the daily ministrations. And the only possible way in which such a growth could have taken place was by direct propaganda—that is to say, by public and private argument and teaching.

It would hardly seem necessary to state so obvious a truth were it not for the fact that Dr. Kirsopp Lake in a widely circulated sentence has lent his name to what appears to be a direct denial that this was the case. The passage in question is as follows:

'Matthew and the Gospel of Peter give us a valuable hint that the story of the empty tomb, and the emphasis which was laid on it, came into discussion at a later period, in connection with the controversy between the Jews and Christians. That this controversy does not belong to the earliest period is psychologically certain. *At the beginning the Jews were not prepared to argue; they persecuted.* Only later, when Christianity had obtained a firm footing, can argument and controversy have begun.'—(Page 195.)

If these words are to be taken literally, they can only mean that at no time in Dr. Lake's view did the 'Jews' argue with the Christians prior to the Great Persecution of A.D. 35; that in some incomprehensible way the movement just grew, without argument or disputation of any kind, until its formidable character attracted the notice of the authorities and drew the expected reprisals.

This is, of course, manifestly absurd—indeed, it is so

133

contrary to the evidence that I cannot believe that Dr. Lake really intends to suggest it. What he means, I take it, is that the highly placed rulers did not *themselves* condescend to argue or dispute with the Christians.

In this they were merely following the tradition of their class, and repeating the tactics they employed against Jesus. Throughout the long drawn-out struggle with Jesus these highly placed Sadducees—the men who really controlled the situation—did not appear. They left it to their sub-ordinates, the Scribes and Pharisees, to debate with, and endeavour to entangle, the Great Teacher. It was only when their arch-enemy was at last actually within their power that Annas, with his son-in-law, Caiaphas and the other members of this wealthy Sadducean family, threw off the mask and came into the open.

So, clearly, it was with the after-history of the movement. Every now and then we find the High Priest and his associates emerging to take official action, such as the summary arrest and interrogation of Peter and John, but for the most part they remain in the background. It has always been a sound maxim of Governments and official persons to avoid playing into the hands of their adversaries by affecting to ignore inconvenient minorities until the pressure of events compels them to do otherwise.

But while it may thus be true that the highly placed representatives of the Jewish hierarchy 'did not argue with the Christians', it is obviously not true of the Jews themselves. It could not possibly be true. Practically every convert to the faith for the first five years was a Jew himself. You could not have a movement growing at an average rate of eighteen to twenty new recruits every week for five years without a ferment of ideas involving both public and private argument. And it is in the character of that argument that the real interest of this story lies.

Now if anyone will sit down and try to reason out quietly how it was that this small body of personal adherents of Jesus grew within four or five years to the dimensions required by the severity of the Great Persecution, he will be increasingly perplexed by one fact—the fact that all this took place within a surprisingly short distance of Joseph's tomb. And whatever may have happened to Joseph himself, this tomb was irremovable. If, therefore, the negative critics were right, we should have the really ironical situation that throughout the period when the disciples were gaining converts daily at a prodigious rate, the conclusive disproof of their main contention lay within two thousand yards of the scene of the controversy, and in the very tomb where everybody knew it had been placed on the afternoon of the Crucifixion.

This, indeed, might have been a quite intelligible situation had the disciples taken almost any other line than that which they did. A moment's reflection will show that many things could be said about Christ during the critical weeks following the Crucifixion without raising, even in a distant connection, the condition of the grave. It could be asserted that He was a great and good man whose violent death in the height of His power was a national calamity and even a national disgrace. It could be contended that the sublime teaching of the Sermon on the Mount, and of the parables, marked Him out as the greatest of the long line of prophets and seers which had been born in Israel. It might even be asserted, though at some risk to one's personal liberty, that the whole prosecution was a deliberate murder, and a heinous offence in the sight of God.

We can imagine any one of these statements being discussed in a private or semi-public meeting in Jerusalem, after the excitable Jewish manner, with much heat and volubility, and then the whole company, so to say, putting on their hats and going home without a single person giving a thought to that silent chamber in Joseph's grotto. But we cannot by any stretch of the imagination conceive of such meetings being held in the very heart of the city, to celebrate and proclaim the *resurrection* of Jesus without the mind of every single hearer going back instantly to the crucial matter of the tomb.

Very subtly, but decisively, the condition of the grave itself would become the final arbiter in this matter. Either it contained the remains of Jesus or it did not. If it did *not* contain the body, one thing is absolutely certain. St. Paul must have been aware of that very surprising fact. He must have known of it from the beginning, through the whole period of his disputations with the Christians—and the Great Persecution must have been deliberately launched in despite of it.

One can hardly imagine a considerable body of people going about Jerusalem and declaring quite openly that Jesus had risen side by side, as it were, with the phenomenon of the empty tomb, without the two circumstances being very widely and publicly connected. The authorities might affect to ignore the disciples' claim, but the fact that the body of a first-class political prisoner had disappeared in mysterious circumstances could not in any conceivable circumstances be unknown to them. And if the authorities knew, Saul would know also.

Thus, if the Marcan narrative is true, Saul of Tarsus must have been abundantly informed concerning the real facts, not only from the official side as regards the supposed abduction of the body, but through his disputations in the Synagogue with the Christian interpretation also. But we are specially concerned at this juncture with the contrary assumption that the Marcan narrative is not true.

We are asked to assume that throughout the entire period when Saul was challenging the Christian party to the first and greatest fight of its existence, and, of course, for many years afterwards, the body of Jesus lay in Joseph's tomb. It follows that when, three years later, he returned to Jerusalem, a converted man, it was still there, and that Saul knew it. We have to think of him spending an entire fortnight at the Christian headquarters conferring chiefly with Peter and James concerning a doctrine in which the fate of the body was of no account. The legend of the women's adventure (in this case a wholly fictitious creation of a secondary epoch) had not yet arisen. The honesty of these men is unimpeached. They had a big enough task already without complicating it by direct falsehoods or imaginary marvels. Their whole problem was how best to preach their unique message to the world. We have to think of them, therefore, gravely discussing policies and plans and recollections with the knowledge that the remains of their Great Master still lay in the tomb.

Was this the historic situation? I suggest that it was not, and that nothing can adjust it and bring it into alignment with the facts. Consider first the small but highly significant fact that not a trace exists in the Acts, or the Missionary Epistles or in any apocryphal document of indisputably early date, of anyone going to pay homage at the shrine of Jesus Christ. It is remarkable—this absolutely unbroken silence concerning the most sacred placc in Christian memory. Would no woman, to whom the Master's form was a hallowed recollection, ever wish to spend a few moments at that holy site? Would Peter and John and Andrew never feel the call of a sanctuary that held all that was mortal of the Great Master? Would Saul himself, recalling his earlier arrogance and self-assurance, not have made one solitary journey and shed hot tears of repentance for his denial of the Name? If these people really knew that the Lord was buried there, it is very, very strange.

Consider next the very singular matter of the documents. The testimony is curiously inverted. It faces strangely in the wrong direction. If Christianity began by proclaiming merely the survival of Jesus, and progressed by slow stages of legendary accretion to belief in the physical vacancy of the tomb, the oldest and most primitive documents ought to be the least emphatic. The clear lamp of the original normality ought to be seen shining through their primitive and archaic language. It is not so. It is precisely the Matthæan and Marcan documents, which by universal consent reach back further towards the lost origins, which are most sharply cut in their outlines, and which describe the vacant tomb with the coldest objectivity.

Consider, too, the infinitely perplexing fact that behind two at least of the synoptic gospels there stands an unshaken historical connection between the probable authors and St. Paul. The man who wrote the 24th chapter of St. Luke spent many weeks in the company of the great apostle. He was more than a companion; he was a friend. In his closing

years St. Paul wrote the immortal tribute to his fidelity:
'Only Luke is with me.'

The man who wrote the first eight verses of the 16th
Chapter of St. Mark was in all human probability, by the
admission of the best modern scholarship, John Mark
himself, a young man who quarrelled with the Apostle
but who lived to regain his affection and regard. Did both
these men secretly hold a doctrine which was opposed to
that of the venerable leader they followed and admired?

Thus, long before we come to the Missionary Letters the
hypothesis gives occasion for the gravest doubt. But when
we turn to the admittedly genuine letters of St. Paul himself
and read them in the only way it is fair to read them, taking
the words in their plain and obvious sense, the last vestige
of uncertainty as to St. Paul's real beliefs concerning the
Resurrection seems to be removed.

Consider, for example, this isolated and almost paren-
thetical reference from the very early letter to the Galatians:

'Paul, an apostle (not from men, neither through man, but
through Jesus Christ, and God the Father, *who raised him from the
dead*).'

Or this from the even earlier First Epistle to the Thessa-
lonians:

'Ye turned unto God from idols, to serve a living and true God,
and *to wait for his Son from heaven, whom he raised from the dead*,
even Jesus, which delivereth us from the wrath to come.'

Or this from the famous introduction to the list of witnesses
in the 15th chapter of First Corinthians:

'For I delivered unto you first of all that which also I received, how
that Christ died for our sins according to the scriptures and that he
was buried; and that *he hath been raised on the third day* according to
the scriptures. . . .'

Or yet again this reference in the same brilliant chapter:

'If Christ is preached that he hath been raised from the dead, how
say some among you that there is no resurrection of the dead?'

It is difficult to read these passages, either with or without their context, without feeling that the writer's thought is far removed from that of mere spiritual survival. But there is one graphic paragraph in this same chapter which surely sets the whole matter at rest.

Like large numbers of his fellow-Christians, St. Paul believed that Jesus of Nazareth would return in glory to the earth, and he clearly expected it in his own lifetime. We need not stay to consider the difficulties which such a concept presents to the modern mind, because it is beside the point. It was a belief which commended itself to vast numbers of people during the first fifty years of the Christian era, and St. Paul shared it.

Now there was a very practical question connected with this belief. Some of the believers had died; others were still living. How was this situation to be met at the return of Christ? St. Paul answers the question with unqualified directness.

'Behold, I tell you a mystery: We shall not all sleep, but we shall all be changed, in a moment, in the twinkling of an eye, at the last trump: for the trumpet shall sound, and the dead shall be raised incorruptible, and we shall be changed.'

It is impossible to take this passage in the obvious sense in which the writer intended it without recognizing that behind it lay a definite concept of the *transmutation* of the physical body into the glorified and spiritual body. It was indeed true, as St. Paul saw very plainly, that mere 'flesh and blood could not inherit the Kingdom'. Something had to happen, both to the dead and the living, to fit them for life in the transcendent sphere. In the case of the dead, St. Paul conceived of this change or transmutation as taking place at the instant of resurrection. But that he conceived the identical body as undergoing this change seems to be indisputable. 'It [the body] is sown in corruption; it is raised in incorruption: it is sown in dishonour; it is raised in glory: it is sown in weakness; it is raised in power: it is sown a natural body; it is raised a spiritual body. If there is a natural body, there is also a spiritual body.' Elsewhere he sharpens this definition to an even finer point when he writes to the Romans that God 'shall quicken your mortal bodies'.

*   *   *   *   *

Thus everything that we know about St. Paul is consistent with the assumption that he believed the tomb of Christ to have been vacant on the morning of Easter Sunday. Nothing that we know about him supports the suggestion that he knew it had never been disturbed.

I cannot find, however, that any modern writer has recognized and worked out the important bearing which the historic phenomena of the grave must have had upon the *conversion* of St. Paul.

It will be apparent to everyone who gives this subject a moment's thought that so completely exhaustive an intellectual conversion as that of St. Paul must have rested, not merely upon a partial acquiescence in one aspect of the disciples' case but on a fundamental satisfaction as to its truth as a whole. Yet volumes have been written upon the psychology of the conversion as though it were a subject which could be discussed quite independently of Saul's thought about the problem of the grave. This problem lay at the core of the whole controversy, and it was clearly impossible for Saul to have reached the point of extreme and violent antipathy to the Christian belief without having his own private opinion concerning it.

Now if the conclusions of our present study be justified the fact was that the tomb was vacant on Sunday morning. I submit that when Saul came upon the scene this fact was not doubted. It never had been. But it was the subject of a bitter difference of opinion between the opposing camps. The Christians asserted that the body had been raised. The Jewish rulers declared that it had been stolen.

It must not be overlooked, however, that Saul entered the fray as a partisan of the Priests. He must have shared their knowledge and taken largely their point of view. If the reader will try to put himself in the place of Saul he will see how difficult it was for a really logical mind to be opposed to the Christians without taking a most sinister view concerning the vacant tomb. The whole thing would look like a 'plant'. He could hardly avoid drawing the conclusion that, even if the disciples themselves had not actually planned it, they were *at least privy to the abduction and concealment of the body*. This lifted the whole thing out of the region of legitimate discussion into the field of deliberate falsehood and deceit. It called for one thing only—its utter and ruthless extermination enforced by the full power of the State.

Thus began the Great Persecution, of which the arrest and stoning of Stephen was the first overt act. That the almost unearthly serenity with which Stephen went to his death left its mark upon the mind of Paul is unquestioned, as indeed it must have done upon many others. But there was no abating of the severity of the onslaught. It was intensified. The haunts of the Christians were systematically raided. Men and women were brought brutally to the State prisons to await summary judgment, followed in many cases by death. Others fled to distant villages, to find themselves pursued by the same implacable hatred and universal power. It became a very dangerous thing to proclaim or admit adhesion to the cause of the Nazarene.

It was while things were in this state that news came to Saul, doubtless from the leaders of the orthodox synagogue at Damascus, that things were not well in that city. The heresy had already taken deep root, and was being strengthened daily by the arrival of fresh fugitives. Saul could not suffer the thought or remain passive so long as any vestige of the conspiracy remained unpunished. He sought and obtained from the Jewish power in Jerusalem letters of authority to the dependent synagogues. Assembling a little party of supporters, he left the city upon the most momentous journey of his life.

Six days later, as the dusty procession came within sight of Damascus, something happened—something destined to have profound and far-reaching effects upon the world's history. There is reason to think that those who accompanied Saul saw a light, other than that produced by the glare of

the noonday sun, and that when they picked him up he
was a temporarily blinded man. We are told that they led
him by the hand for the short distance that separated them
from the city. It was a strange ending to so brave and determined an adventure, but I do not see that we can doubt
that it is historic. St. Luke could surely not have obtained
the very circumstantial details which he gives from anyone
else than St. Paul himself.

How can we account for this incident having the admittedly historical consequences that it did! Why should a
man of this tough breed and of this admittedly sane and
virile mental calibre be uprooted in an instant from his
cherished beliefs and swept like chaff before the wind into
the dogmatic camp of his most hated enemies?

It is not the immediate effects of the conversion with
which we are concerned, though these are noteworthy. But
how did this reorientation of a man's entire presuppositions
survive the three years' solitary communion in Arabia, and
the nine years' patient waiting in Tarsus, and all the bitter
persecutions and hardships of the great missions? Why was
one of the greatest intellects of the ages brought over and
fixed in an instant of time from one pole of dogmatic belief
to another?

We do not know, and shall probably never know, all that
Saul experienced on the Damascus road. There are many
ways in which invisible reality can make itself known and
felt to the sentient soul of man. But of one thing I am personally convinced. The facts which converted Saul were the
same facts which so profoundly modified the behaviour of
Peter and Matthias and James the Just—but, curiously, they
came to him in the reverse order.

The disciples began with the staggering but confusing fact
of the empty tomb. It was one of the physical surprises of
that memorable morning. There is reason to believe that
they were actively sought after by the authorities on that
account, and that when they met it was behind locked doors.

But with St. Paul the situation was strangely different. He
came to the whole singular phenomenon from the opposite
point of the compass. He was saturated with the priestly

point of view. To him the disciples, like their Master, were deceivers, blasphemers against God, and the authors of a wicked and dangerous heresy. He was determined to stamp it out to the last man. He started for Damascus with that intent. He arrived there an utterly shaken and repentant man. Nothing that he saw or heard or experienced thereafter had the slightest effect upon this settled state of mind. He recovered from his temporary blindness; he did not recover either his scepticism or his hate. He went into Arabia for many months in solitary seclusion to think it out. He came back the same radically altered man. He was ready to preach in Damascus, and did preach, but his name spelt terror to his late enemies, and some friendly spirits let him down in a basket over the rampart of the city. He had the courage to go to Jerusalem and face the ignominy, the contempt of his return. He spent fifteen days with Peter, who knew as much as any mortal man could know about the whole matter. Again he was smuggled out of the city to avoid trouble, and returned to his native Tarsus.

And yet, when nine years later, the young Church at Antioch, remembering his zeal, sent Barnabas to fetch him, they found a man utterly unchanged in the serenity and fixity of his belief. As we read the letters of his middle and later life we find no trace of any mental weakening, rather the coming to maturity of a fine intellect, an intensely logical and ordered mind.

I have purposely stated the essential facts very soberly because the facts themselves are sober. You cannot explain a lifetime's practical devotion like this by 'atmospherics' or providential thunderstorms or any ephemeral or hysterical experience. If it requires a 'purple passage' to describe how St. Paul came to believe in Christ, we may be certain that we are on the wrong track.

It may indeed be that the actual experience which came to him on the Damascus road was in some way peculiar and conditioned by his temperament. It may be, as Dr. Lake himself has hinted, that an invisible Presence really did stand at that roadside, and that as Saul drew near he saw something which animals sometimes seem to sense, rather than to apprehend with the physical eye. It may even be that he heard a voice. Have we never heard our own name spoken with the utmost plainness and distinctness when no mortal person was present? It is not really strange that according to his companions, they heard Saul speaking, and looking round saw no one.

In such questions we touch the very borderline of our present knowledge. But on the intellectual side of this phenomenon the truth is clear. When Saul was really convinced that he had seen the risen Jesus the immense and overpowering significance of the empty tomb swept for the first time into his mind. It was as though the great stone itself had crashed into and carried away his last defences. He saw that if the disciples were not deceivers, they then were *right*—right through the whole range and gamut of their claim. He realized why you could not associate a martyrdom so glorious as that of Stephen with a vulgar deception involving connivance with the abduction of a corpse. He began to understand why Peter was so sure, and why everyone connected with this movement was so unaccountably joyous and so immovably convinced.

And the curious thing is—indeed, it is the master circumstance of all this strange story—that once this conviction has been reached, its effect upon any normally constituted mind was enduring. The vacancy of the tomb was an historic fact—fixed and unalterable. Its authority grew rather than declined with the passing of the years. It was never shaken throughout St. Paul's lifetime, and in the writer's judgment it remains unshaken to this day.

Chapter XIII

THE WITNESS OF THE GREAT STONE

I suppose that no one can read through the earliest account of the Resurrection as it is given in the Gospel of St. Mark without being arrested by the extraordinary significance of what we are told about the golal or great stone which according to the evidence was placed against the entrance to the grave.

We are all familiar with the kind of shock a man experiences when he encounters suddenly something for which he is not looking, something which, like the footprint on the sand in Crusoe's story, sends the mind swiftly back in search of an explanation. Such an experience, I think, awaits everyone who comes freshly to the story as it is told in St. Mark, because contrary to expectation and without searching for it we are driven by the logic of the facts to investigate another story, told in another Gospel, the story of the *guards*.

I remember with some vividness the surprise with which this fact was first borne in upon my own mind, because I had fallen into the habit of regarding the reported incident of the guard as being of a secondary and probably apologetic character. The general trend of critical opinion was then, as now, somewhat unfavourable to its acceptance as a genuine fact of history. It was pointed out that it was an unheard-of thing for soldiers, particularly Roman soldiers, to sleep at their post of duty; that even if they declared they had done so nobody would have believed them; and finally, that the reasons given for posting a guard at all were in themselves highly improbable and belong to a later and secondary epoch.

I accepted these statements at the time without question and proceeded entirely upon the hypothesis that no one troubled to go to the grave between sunset on Friday and the hour when the women put in an appearance. The implication was that neither the Romans nor the Priests took any interest in the tomb of Christ after the latter had once been assured that the law demanding burial before sunset had been complied with.

To my surprise I found that the teaching of the Marcan record (the only really early account of the Resurrection we possess) does not wholly support this view, but is rather to the opposite effect. In order that we may consider closely all that it implies, it will be helpful to have the full text of the Marcan passage before us right up to the point where the original manuscript breaks off:

'And when the sabbath was past, Mary Magdalene, and Mary the mother of James, and Salome, bought spices, that they might come and anoint him. And very early on the first day of the week, they come to the tomb when the sun was risen. And they were saying among themselves, Who shall roll us away the stone from the door of the tomb? and looking up, they see that the stone is rolled back: for it was exceeding great. And entering into the tomb, they saw a young man sitting on the right side, arrayed in a white robe; and they were amazed. And he saith unto them, Be not amazed; ye seek Jesus, the Nazarene, which hath been crucified: he is risen; he is not here: behold, the place where they laid him! But go, tell his disciples and Peter, He goeth before you into Galilee: there shall ye see him, as he said unto you. And they went out, and fled from the tomb; for trembling and astonishment had come upon them: and they said nothing to any one; for they were afraid. . . .'

This is the incomparable original fragment which has descended to us. It is by far the oldest and most authoritative account of what happened to the women, and it probably follows closely the story as they related it and as it was first circulated in primitive times.

First a word as to its atmosphere. It is impossible to read this passage impartially and with an open mind without being impressed, and impressed favourably, by its straightforward and objective character. It is singularly frank, open, and direct. It shows few, if any, traces of adjustment to later conceptions. It is primitive in character and nails the original version of the episode, as it were, to the mast. Moreover, and this is a point of considerable significance, it is entirely free from incidents of a necessarily supernormal character. It tells of the women setting out to arrive at the tomb about dawn. It describes their anxiety concerning the stone. It tells how on reaching the tomb and finding the stone already moved they went in and found a young man sitting within in a white garment. It tells how he gave them a certain message which in their highly strung and unprepared state unnerved them so that they fled in confusion from the tomb.

This is of course very dramatic and unusual, but the whole story is unusual, from the sudden arrest and crucifixion of Jesus to His hurried burial in a rich man's grave. Given the early hour, the half-light, the uncanny feeling which is associated with all human contacts with the dead, and the utter unpreparedness of the women for what actually happened, their behaviour in the circumstances described is strikingly realistic and true to life.

But, as I have said, it is with the stone itself that we are chiefly concerned—the one silent and infallible witness in the whole episode—and there are certain facts about this stone which call for very careful study and investigation.

Let us begin by considering first its size and probable character. The passage which I have quoted above leaves us in no doubt that the stone was large and consequently very heavy. This fact is asserted or implied by all the writers who refer to it. St. Mark says it was 'exceeding great'. St. Matthew speaks of it as 'a great stone'. 'Peter' says, 'for the stone was great'. Additional testimony on this point is furnished by the reported anxiety of the women as to how they should move it. If the stone had not been of considerable weight the combined strength of three women should have been capable of moving it. We receive, therefore, a very definite impression that it was at least too weighty for the women to remove unaided. All this has a very definite bearing upon the case, as we shall see shortly.

Now the fact which is stated with great explicitness in all the surviving versions of the incident is that when the women arrived at the tomb they found that the stone had been moved.

I do not think that the physical implications of this fact have been fully realized. For surely it means that the women were not first at the tomb. They were forestalled. Someone who had a very definite interest in this tomb had been there prior to their arrival. That this is the only possible inference for those who believe, as I do, that we are here on the track of a true historic event will be obvious.

Unless, therefore, we are prepared to maintain that the stone was moved by supernatural agency, or that it was pushed forward from within, or that it became displaced accidentally by an earth tremor (a contingency in Judea not wholly to be set aside), it becomes a matter of great historical importance to know what person or persons had both the opportunity and the incentive to disturb it. For it is clear that as early as dawn on Sunday morning it had been moved.

This is a very big and formidable inquiry, involving the re-opening of some questions which we have already considered. But I see no means of avoiding it. If the visit of the women is historic, the fact that the stone had been interfered with is historic also. We must, therefore, accept it as one of the physical conditions of our inquiry.

Let us consider in turn the three principal directions from which such an interference with the grave might have come. Could Joseph of Arimathea have returned after all, as he clearly had the right to do some time between the close of the Sabbath observance and the moment when the women came upon the scene?

The answer to this question must clearly depend upon the purpose for which he came. If it is contended that he came privily and alone (let us say to have a final look at the features of the dead Leader), then I think we must reject the suggestion decisively on two counts. In the first place it is most improbable that he would have done this in the middle of the night. Secondly, the evidence is that *he would not have been able to get in*. If three women felt themselves unable to move the stone, on the ground of its great size and weight, it would require at least two men to have done so.

Joseph, if he came alone, would have been barred out of the tomb by his own act.

We are left, therefore, with the suggestion that Joseph came with a working party, choosing, perhaps, the dark hours to avoid the curious attentions of the crowd, and with the express object of removing the body to a more suitable resting-place. I have always felt that, if no other satisfactory solution offered, this would have to rank high as a purely rationalistic explanation of the observed phenomena. It falls in with two elements of the situation very aptly. It explains why the women found the tomb open. It also explains why we cannot locate the body.

But it runs aground irretrievably at this point. It does not explain why, when a few weeks later Jerusalem was ringing with the claim that Jesus had risen and had been seen by His disciples, the men who helped Joseph to perform this nocturnal exhumation and reburial, did not declare what they knew. The alternative tomb could not have been very far away, and it is doubtful whether the re-interment could have been accomplished at all without some kind of official permit.

Moreover, there is the *bona-fides* of Joseph himself to consider in the matter. If it is true that Joseph acted in a sense on behalf of the Jewish authorities, in fulfilling the law by burying the body before sunset, what possible reason could there be for concealing this perfectly natural and legal proceeding? Annas and Caiaphas and the other leaders behind the prosecution must have been privy to it. If so, why their silence, when the mere statement of the fact, supported by irrefragable proofs, would have been the most damning and conclusive reply to the pretensions of the Christians?

But there is another and a very serious point where the hypothesis fails to join on with the recorded evidence. It throws no light whatever upon the women's assertion in the earliest and most primitive record that they found someone in occupation of the tomb.

Those critics who have fastened upon the fact that in the Marcan account there is nothing necessarily supernormal in the identity of this 'young man' seem to me to render real service to the cause of truth. A statement so matter-of-fact and circumstantial as this would hardly falter upon the fundamental objective element of the situation. If the evidence is strong that the women went to the tomb and found it open, it seems to me equally strong that they encountered and were spoken to by someone when they reached there.

Yet by no conceivable fancy can we imagine Joseph and his party taking the precaution to leave anyone behind in the tomb when it was once vacated. They would almost certainly require the whole of their personnel to carry out the operation in hand. To leave a picket in the tomb for any purpose whatever seems outside the requirements of the situation. What with the necessity of carrying lights and tools and the need for resting the bier as they went along, even a party of three people would have their hands pretty full. Moreover, the reported message given to the women is utterly at variance with what such a picket, in such circumstances, would have said. It seems therefore that we must reject the hypothesis as being contrary to the available evidence.

We come now to the second group in our inquiry—the friends and disciples of Jesus. I said in an earlier chapter of this book that, by the almost universal consent of mankind, it was unthinkable that these overwrought and harassed people should have had either the originality or the daring to have conceived and carried out this feat. Since then we have studied the behaviour of these people closely at short range, and the previous decision stands. It stands impregnably on moral grounds alone. Anything seems preferable to the supposition that the disciples either singly or as a party were capable of such a deception, and the conversion of Saul clinches it. Saul came over at last because he was convinced not only that the disciples were honest, but that they were right!

Thus by a process of exhaustion we come to our third group, the Jewish authorities themselves, and here the field widens, because, when we think of it, there are a number of reasons why the official power might have taken an interest in this tomb *during the particular period which we are considering*.

The modern critical distrust of the story of the guards seems to be based upon certain doubts arising mainly under two distinct headings:

1. That the story bears marks of being apologetic in character and therefore belongs probably to a later age than that in which the Christian crusade was launched.
2. That it is improbable in itself and is inconsistent with the ascertained realities of the situation.

We will agree at once, that, if in later years the Christians were pressed for a really indisputable proof of their contention, a story of this concrete kind would go far to allay doubt and to steady the faith of the nascent Church. But this of course would equally be the case if the story were true or had a substantial substratum of truth in it. The whole thing really turns upon two questions: Is it improbable in itself? Is it inconsistent with the other known facts of the situation? After careful consideration it seems to me that to both questions we must return a decided negative.

As everyone knows, there are three versions of the story of the guard preserved in the early literature, and these accounts differ materially in certain details. In St. Matthew, which is of course by far the earliest and generally the most trustworthy document, the guards tell their story to the Priests and are paid by them to circulate a false statement. In 'Peter' the guards report direct to Pilate, and are told by him to keep silence. In 'Nicodemus' they follow the course described by St. Matthew.

But *all* the accounts are in fundamental agreement upon two points:

1. That Pilate was approached and gave permission for such a guard to be set.
2. That the guard kept watch during the night preceding the visit of the women.

Now the reported approach to Pilate is very significant. The position of the Jews in relation to the remains of Jesus was peculiar, and in a certain sense delicate. Although He was a Jew and had been prosecuted at the instance of the Jewish leaders, the punishment and sentence was Roman. Technically, the body of Jesus was Roman property and the disposal of it a Roman concern. After the rebuff they had received over the wording of the superscription, this was no time for appearing to override Pilate's authority or even to appear to be encroaching upon Roman preserves. If, therefore, the Priests had any real concern with the tomb of Christ, it seems certain that they would be compelled first to communicate their anxieties to Pilate, and through him to gain freedom to do what they considered necessary.

All this points strongly to the truth of the story, because in later years this purely technical sovereignty of Pilate over the crucified body would tend to be overlooked. It is only a small point, but to the trained student of history the synchronization between the report and the less noticeable requirements of a situation is instructive.

This brings us to the question: had the Priests a strong incentive, or indeed any incentive at all, to concern themselves about the tomb of Christ? Was this incentive sufficient to justify the possible raising of further trouble by going to the Procurator? Pilate was admittedly in a bad humour, and discretion dictated giving him a wide berth. Is there anything of a sufficiently urgent character to warrant us in believing that they went to him a second time?

Those who assert that there is not, surely overlook two very considerable elements in the situation. In the first place there are strong reasons for thinking that some kind of temporary guard or watch must inevitably have been placed over this particular garden. Had the body of Jesus been cast, as might have been expected, into the common grave, official protection for the burial-place would naturally have been provided as a matter of course. Jerusalem was always a very crowded and turbulent place at feast times, and this was no ordinary execution. You could not have so famous and in some quarters so execrated a body as that of Jesus, lying about, as it were, in a place accessible to the public without let or hindrance. It is absurd to suppose anything so foreign to the highly civilized government which Jerusalem possessed. The precautions appropriate to the occasion would have been provided automatically, and no one would have thought it in any way unusual.

But if there is one bit of historic truth which stands out of the narratives it is that the body of Jesus did not suffer this particular indignity. All the documents declare that Joseph of Arimathea, a Jew of some local standing and substance, went to Pilate and 'asked for the body', and that Pilate granted this request. Joseph of Arimathea thereupon proceeded with his plans, using a tomb which may have been chosen owing to its near proximity to the Cross, but which more probably was his own personal and private property.

I do not think, however, that it has been fully realized how this simple circumstance, unimportant though it may appear at first sight, must have altered the whole legal and constitutional position with regard to the body of Jesus in so far as it affected the maintenance of law and order in Jerusalem.

The onus of keeping the peace and of maintaining order among the vast throngs which came to the feasts, rested entirely upon the civil power. Had Jesus been convicted of any offence less serious than that involving the capital sentence, His safe custody and protection would have fallen solely to the Jewish authorities. But the Roman Emperor had expressly removed the power to inflict the *death sentence* from sectarian hands. Thus with the uttering of Pilate's judgment, the legal control of the Prisoner passed definitely from the Great Sanhedrin and its officers into the Roman charge. Technically, at least, Pilate was responsible for the consequences of his own act.

This would doubtless have suited the High Priest and his advisers very well, because had any unruly demonstrations taken place, either at the place of Crucifixion or of subsequent burial, the Procurator himself would quickly have suppressed them, if necessary by armed force.

But history did not take this particular course. To the intense dismay and indignation of the authorities, one of their own number went privately to Pilate and begged the body. This reversed the whole favourable position from the priestly point of view and brought the protection of the grave and the maintenance of public order definitely back again as a strictly Jewish and official concern. Hence the fury of the authorities against Joseph which is so plainly indicated in the apocryphal literature.

Even, therefore, if no hint had been given to us in the Gospels that such was the case, we should have been compelled to assume that the question of preserving order under the quite exceptional conditions created by the proceedings against Christ gave the High Priest and his advisers occasion for some disquiet. Pilate, in the most open way possible, had washed his hands for the second time of all responsibility in the matter of the Nazarene. He had delivered the body to the care of a Jew, who buried it (possibly from necessity) in a peculiarly open and exposed place beyond the city gate. If trouble or rioting occurred at the place of burial, the responsibility for quelling it would have been the Priests', and Pilate would have been quick to emphasize that constitutional point.

Obviously the simplest way out of their dilemma was for the Priests to go to Pilate with a request that the military authorities themselves should undertake temporarily the protection of the Garden. This was the more reasonable since Pilate undoubtedly had the necessary reserves while Caiaphas could only fall back upon the Temple Guard— a quite inadequate force in the event of really dangerous trouble arising. That the Priests did go to Pilate with this very natural request, but with wholly unexpected results, seems to be clear from the Gospel according to St. Matthew.

The passage in which St. Matthew describes what took place at this interview is very instructive, and it will be helpful to have the exact words before us:

'Now on the morrow, which is the day after the Preparation, the chief priests and the Pharisees were gathered together unto Pilate, saying, Sir, we remember that that deceiver said, while he was yet alive, After three days I rise again. Command therefore that the sepulchre be made sure until the third day, lest haply his disciples come and steal him away, and say unto the people, He is risen from the dead: and the last error will be worse than the first. Pilate said unto them, Ye have a guard: go your way, make it as sure as ye can. So they went, and made the sepulchre sure, sealing the stone, the guard being with them.'

Such is the earliest, and unquestionably the purest form in which this persistent old tradition has come down to us.

If the reader will concentrate his attention in the first instance upon the matters of fact recorded in this passage, he will find that there are four definite statements:

1. That the interview took place, *not on the day of the Crucifixion*, but the day after. This is given quite explicitly: 'On the morrow, which is the day after the Preparation.'
2. That Pilate was expressly asked to undertake the protection of the tomb: 'Command therefore that the sepulchre be made sure.'
3. That Pilate *refused this request*: 'Ye have a guard: go your way, make it as sure as ye can.'
4. That the priests thereupon acted upon their own initiative: 'So they went and made the sepulchre sure, sealing the stone, the guard being with them.'

This is a perfectly reasonable and logical sequence of events. It fits in with a situation of immediate and pressing anxiety to the Priests; it agrees with the known character of Pilate; and it explains why the women had no occasion to alter their plans.

It is frequently asserted by modern writers upon this subject that it is 'impossible to find room' for the incident of the guard in the earliest tradition. The suggestion is that, had the women known that the tomb was guarded, they would not have set out upon their secret mission.

So long as the guard is loosely thought of as being set with full public knowledge throughout the whole period of the temporary burial, it will of course be impossible to find room for the visit of the women. But according to St. Matthew it was not set in this spectacular and melodramatic way. Its necessity was not recognized for nearly twenty-four hours after Joseph had laid the body in the tomb. It was only when the Sabbath was drawing to a close, and the city was about to reawaken to its normal life that the extreme urgency of this matter seems to have been recognized. How could three or four women be expected to know what was going on secretly at the Procurator's residence on Saturday evening, especially if, as is most probable, they went to bed early in preparation for their work at dawn?

Secondly, the point which is usually urged against the probability of the Priests taking action in this matter seems to me to be open to very serious doubt. It is usually contended that the excuse given to Pilate (viz. that the disciples might steal the body) is wildly improbable; that even if it could be conclusively proved that Jesus predicted His resurrection, the behaviour of the disciples shows that they had not apprehended or believed Him; and the elaborate setting of an official guard to prevent such a shadowy contingency is, to say the least, unlikely.

Personally, I should feel the force of this argument very strongly *if it agreed with the accounts of the Trial*, which it does not. It seems to me a very strange and suggestive thing that right back in the very earliest and most primitive accounts of this trial there is the persistent assertion that the whole case against Jesus hinged upon a sentence containing those cryptic and most unusual words: 'in three days'.

We are not dealing with unsophisticated or half-educated people in this very able bit of political statecraft, but with some of the subtlest and most observant Jewish intellects of their day. Behind all their manœuvring for position, the search for actual witnesses, and the sudden dropping of the charge when the witnesses failed to agree together, is the evident historical fact that Jesus on some memorable occasion made use of a phrase containing these words, a phrase which clearly infuriated the Sadducean leaders, but which would not stand the literal meaning which the witnesses tried to give to it.

If, therefore, as the records plainly show, the main attack of the prosecution was concentrated upon this phrase, the inference seems to be clear. Not only did Jesus make a statement which is probably preserved in its fullness in St. John, but the Priests knew that He had made it and deliberately selected it as the most vulnerable utterance for their purpose.

All this produces a situation involving the exact opposite of *indifference* to the conditions of His interment. No one at that early stage could predict what was happening in the minds of the vast multitudes who, a few days previously, had hailed Jesus as their political deliverer. To leave the tomb utterly unprotected, when a reasonably urgent request to Pilate would ensure it against unauthorized violation by interested persons, was in a measure to invite the very thing which they were most anxious to avoid.

I mention these considerations—not indeed as proof that the guard was set, for such proof is at this distance of time impossible—but to show that the placing of *some kind of watch over the tomb* during this particular and very critical week-end is by no means so improbable as it at first seems.

When, however, we come to consider seriously the consistency of the story with the established facts of the situation, we are on firmer and more positive ground, for surely the biggest and most certain of the ascertained realities in this situation is that some time between the hour when Joseph and his burial-party left the scene and the first streaks of dawn on Sunday, the stone was moved. As from previous observation three women had reasons for doubting whether their combined strength would be equal to the task, the inference is that the party responsible for this action consisted of two or more persons. The time was almost certainly during the dark hours between sunset on Saturday and sunrise on Sunday, for there is no trace of anything unusual on Saturday, and the discovery was made as early as dawn on Sunday.

Thus we seem compelled to postulate the presence near the tomb during the dark hours of Sunday morning of a group of people capable of removing the stone. If the people who did this strange thing were the representatives of the Jewish power, it must have been because some unusual circumstance caused them to look inside the tomb. Moreover, as an hour or so later they were not found by the women, the further inference is that they had gone away to report to their superiors.

These inferences are necessarily provisional, based upon the assumption that it was the watchers who removed the stone. It is of course possible to suggest a quite different solution. If the reader feels that the evidence for the existence of the guard is insufficient, it is open for him to consider whether some other body of people might not have come during the dark hours with far more sinister intent. This is our old solution of the stealing of the body with a vengeance, and with all its collateral consequences. To pursue this idea thoroughly, we should have to inquire what persons there were in Jerusalem at this time who had the necessary incentive to attempt this abduction, what they expected to gain by it, and to what destination and for what purpose they conveyed the body.

But I propose a more radical test than this. It seems to me that no theory concerning these events can be regarded as historically valid which does not simultaneously explain— not only the coming of the women at the time they did, and their finding of the tomb open, but also their dramatic confrontation by the young man in the tomb, and the message which, according to St. Mark, he gave to them.

There is nothing in the passage printed on page 146 to show that the women regarded this individual as a supernormal being. He is just a young man wearing a white garment. They discover him in the tomb and in reply to the question which their dumbfounded appearance clearly suggested, he gives them a curious reply:

'Be not amazed; ye seek Jesus, the Nazarene, which hath been crucified: he is risen; he is not here: behold, the place where they laid him! But go, tell his disciples and Peter, He goeth before you into Galilee: there shall ye see him, as he said unto you.'

So long as the reader allows his mind to be influenced by the fact that in the later and derivative documents these, or closely similar words, are attributed to an angel he will miss much of their force. An angel would naturally be regarded as omniscient and his knowledge would therefore convey little. But directly we think of this young man as an ordinary human being suddenly surprised in his examination of the tomb by the arrival of the women and surprising them in turn by his unexpected presence, light begins to spread over the whole field.

To realize what this dramatic situation means I think it is necessary to try to visualize how the women suddenly and unexpectedly came upon the scene. We have to think of them approaching the tomb in the dim light of the early morning utterly unsuspecting any human presence. Their minds were preoccupied with the stone and how they should move it, and their sole thought was to wrench this away and thus gain access to the dear lacerated body of their Lord.

We do not know how far away they were when the fact that something had changed first became apparent to them, but the probability is that they were quite close. In any case the stone was not where they had last seen it. It was moved to one side and the mouth of the cave stood revealed. The realization of this fact probably halted them for a moment, and then, wondering greatly as to what this might mean, they softly approached the tomb. To their terror they saw a figure sitting in the dark interior, and in the grip of an un- nameable fear they started backwards. Simultaneously the occupant of the tomb, his attention suddenly aroused by the sound of voices outside and the momentary darken- ing of the door, turned round to find them already retiring in alarm.

I picture him running out and *calling* to them as they retreated: 'Don't be frightened. You seek Jesus, the Naza- rene. He is not here. Behold the place where they laid him. . . .' But the women were too terrified and shaken to hold parley, and as Mark graphically states: 'They went out and fled from the tomb; for trembling and astonishment had come upon them.'

If this strange scene was enacted in the manner briefly suggested above, it is clear that we are in the presence of a new and very important fact. The situation is complicated by an independent visitor to the grave who for some reason started even earlier than the women and yet without knowledge of their quest.

Is this person historic or is he a myth? If the former, how does his presence at this particular juncture fit in with and adjust itself to the other known facts of the situation?

Before we consider what the Marcan testimony really is upon this vital question, there is one point which calls for special consideration. I mean the *terror* of the women—that which made them run and flee from the tomb. I do not think that this psychological element of terror in the Marcan record has received the close study it deserves. Setting out as they did with the express purpose of ministering to the dead, the minds of the women must have been prepared in advance for the depressing and even eerie conditions under which the work was to be accomplished. We cannot readily imagine them being alarmed by the vacant chamber or by any creature of their own imagination.

But if you will try to think of three quite ordinary and normally courageous women going to a grave at early dawn with the object of anointing the dead; if you will think of them entering the tomb rather hesitatingly, expecting to find a recumbent corpse in its winding sheet, and finding a *white-robed figure sitting up*, you have all the constituents of terror in their most affrighting form. Few women could have experienced it without running for their lives. And the impression that the Marcan account gives is that they did run, without waiting to consider the full purport of the news that the young man called after them. Such at least is my personal reading of the event. It answers to something deeply necessary to the understanding of the whole story.

But at what cost do we get this glimpse of the strange realities of that morning? For if this young man is an historic feature of the situation, his presence introduces a new factor to the problem, another thread in the web of circumstance which finds its centre and focus in the tomb of Christ. Is there any hypothesis which will explain simultaneously all these unusual and apparently disconnected happenings?

Now it is one of the very curious features of this problem that what seems to be the true answer to these questions is imbedded in the Marcan fragment itself. The clue is provided by the last five words of the message which the young man is reported to have given to the women: 'He goeth before you into Galilee: there shall ye see him, *as he said unto you.*' When did Jesus tell His disciples He would meet them in Galilee? We turn back over the pages of the manuscript, past the account of the trial and the Crucifixion, until we come upon them suddenly in St. Mark.

'And Jesus saith unto them, All ye shall be offended: for it is written, I will smite the shepherd, and the sheep shall be scattered abroad. Howbeit, after I am raised up, I will go before you into Galilee.'

The peculiar thing about this little fragment of conversation is that it is reported to have taken place on the way to Gethsemane. The Paschal Supper was over. Judas had long since left to complete his compact with the Priests. The party, now reduced to eleven men and their Leader, had risen from their couches and descended to the street. It was during the journey to the Garden that Jesus, according to St. Mark, uttered these strange words.

If they were actually uttered, *could they have been overheard?* At first blush we should say 'No!' The very meeting-place for this supper had been kept a close secret by Jesus, lest a premature betrayal should rob Him of that last quiet conference with His friends.

We picture the light being turned out and the party descending quietly and unostentatiously to the street, preparatory to the walk to Gethsemane. There does not seem room for the intrusion of a stranger, or even a sympathizer who was not a member of the Apostolic band.

And yet ... and yet ... according to St. Mark there was at least one other person who made the journey to the Garden of Gethsemane that night. I cannot personally see how the language which St. Mark uses concerning this person can be interpreted in any other way than that he entered the Garden with the disciples, for the narrative clearly says 'he followed *with*' Jesus. And the story about him is meaningless except as an elemental bit of truth, an episode incongruous enough in relation to its setting, but part of the immortal adventure of that night.

I said something in an earlier chapter about the Gospel of St. Mark standing like a great rock far out to sea in advance of the distinctively Christian literature. It arrests even the uncritical reader by the granite sharpness of its detail. And nowhere do we feel its realism more than in that strangely graphic description of the last hour of Christ's freedom. This is surely no merely literary creation of a secondary age. Who would have invented that story of the disciples falling to sleep out of sheer weariness in the gravest hour of their Master's peril; or that touch about the twice-repeated awakening as He returned softly to them at intervals from His communing under the distant trees; or His permissive words, when His personal crisis was past and the peace of decision had come to him: 'Sleep on now, and take your rest', to be followed shortly, as the glare of the advancing torches became visible, 'Arise, let us be going: behold, he that betrayeth me is at hand'?

This is obviously a true history of that never-to-be-forgotten night. It spares no feelings, least of all those of the disciples themselves. It stands out as a stark and imperishable record of one of the master episodes of human history. And if there be one thing which clinches and confirms the veracity of the narrative it is surely that curiously irrelevant incident of the young man whose cloak was snatched from him in the struggle and who fled naked into the night. Why should we be told anything about this man except for the weighty and sufficient reason that the thing happened? The retreating figure of this naked youth is clearly one of the ineffaceable impressions of a dramatic five minutes which remained engraven deeply in the memory of everyone present.

Now there is something infinitely strange in all this, and worthy of the closest study. For the strangeness lies in the way in which certain fixed and unalterable features of the situation fit together.

If anyone will take the story of the women's adventure as it is recorded by St. Mark, and regard it, not as a piece of moonshine, but as an honest and authentic bit of history, he will find himself increasingly impressed by something which does not emerge in the traditional interpretations of the episode. The arresting thing in that story is not that the women went to the tomb at dawn, or even that they found it vacated. It is surely that they were not the first to make the journey that morning; that they were anticipated by some-one who had an equal interest in the tomb, and who had apparently set out from Jerusalem a few minutes earlier than themselves.

This seems to be the obvious meaning of this very ancient and primitive fragment. There is not the slightest hint or suggestion of anything supernatural in the presence of this young man, as St. Mark relates the story. He is merely a fourth party in an unusual adventure. He was probably as much surprised by the arrival of the women as they were startled and terrified by his presence. The swiftness of their recoil on discovering him within the chamber accounts for the brevity of his message, for as I picture the scene, he had to call loudly after them as they were retreating hurriedly from the grave. But the words which he did call after them are perfectly intelligible and surprisingly appropriate to such an occasion. He could not say more, for by that time they were probably out of hearing.

Directly we begin to think of this young man, not as an imaginary visitant from the skies, but as a solid reality of that never-to-be-forgotten morning, we get a situation of extraordinary interest.

We know why the women went to the tomb at this early hour. It was a matter of prearrangement. The expedition was apparently planned on Friday afternoon and prepared for during Saturday. Promptly at the appointed hour, as dawn was breaking over the Eastern hills, the little party moved off upon its sad errand.

But what could have induced a young Hebrew, who pre-sumably had also spent the night in Jerusalem, to go out at an even earlier hour to see the tomb of Christ? The question is worth pondering, for the situation is very peculiar. If the evidence had been that the grave of Jesus was undisturbed when the women came to it, we should be hard pressed to find

163

an intelligible reason why a solitary young man should have set out before dawn on a chilly April morning to go to it. But the evidence is precisely to the opposite effect, and it is overwhelming in its consistency and strength. If one solid bit of real truth about that far-distant morning has come down to us through the ages it is that, to their great surprise, the women found the grave open, and the big stone moved to one side.

This fact, if fact it be, has certain unavoidable implications. It implies in the first instance that the tomb must have been in this state for some little time. The evidence is that the stone was too heavy to have been moved by a single pair of hands, and there is no trace of the women meeting any body of men who were capable of moving it. Whoever moved the stone, therefore, had presumably left the vicinity of the grave earlier in the morning and while it was still dark.

So much lies upon the surface of the situation. But the implication is wider and more far-reaching than that for we have to account not only for the moving of the stone, but the arousing of a young man in Jerusalem to such a pitch of excitement and curiosity that he lost no time in going personally to the grave, arriving there apparently a few minutes before the women. All this is highly significant, because the only way in which anyone in Jerusalem could have known that something unusual had taken place at the grave of Jesus *before* the women reached it, was by the direct report of someone who had just returned. And curiously enough, the only people who exactly fit this description are the guards of the Gospels!

Had the tomb of Jesus been rifled by a band of common marauders, or by people with sinister designs upon the body, they would have disappeared as silently and mysteriously as they came. Certainly they would not have advertised their crime in the streets of Jerusalem within a few minutes of having committed it. Had Joseph of Arimathea, shortly before dawn, opened the cave with a view to removing the remains to another resting-place he would have been still engaged at the new point of sepulture, and any message that he brought would have been reserved ultimately for official ears.

But if, as the darkest hour of night began to turn softly to the grey of dawn, a party of excited men broke into the narrow streets of the old city declaring that something was amiss with the tomb of the Nazarene, then one does indeed begin to understand how more than one sleeper might have been drawn from his bed to discover what this unaccustomed commotion was about and to hear something of the purport of the strange conversations which ensued. And if among those who listened, or to whom swift rumour came by other means, there was one man who had made that perilous journey to the Garden of Gethsemane and had heard those strange words fall from the lips of Christ, who shall describe with what haste he would seize whatever clothing was near at hand, and rushing forth run, as only an intensely moved and excited man could run, to the Garden of the Resurrection?

Chapter XIV

SOME REALITIES OF THAT
FAR-OFF MORNING

What is the secret of this silent and impenetrable tomb? It is a question which presses insistently for an answer, and I propose to discuss it in the present chapter.

There are certain things about this story which impress me profoundly. They are not the kind of things which can lightly be set aside as of minor or only relative importance. They belong to the fundamental and bedrock features of the problem. In the first place, whatever the physical or dogmatic consequences may be, I cannot and do not believe that the body of Jesus of Nazareth rested in Joseph's garden during any part of that period which is contemporary with the rise of Christianity.

If it could be shown that there was a single document of admittedly early date dealing with the crucifixion and burial of Jesus in which it was even remotely hinted that such was the case, I for one should attach to that hint very considerable weight. It would at least introduce the same kind of uncertainty which exists concerning certain other aspects of the problem. It would provide a peg, however shaky and insecure, upon which to hang a doubt. But the documents are adamant upon this fundamental feature of the Easter dawn.

Whether we turn to the two dependent Gospels, St. Matthew and St. Luke, to the comparatively unorthodox Gospel of Peter, to the Gospel of St. John, to the Emmaus document preserved by St. Luke, or to the admittedly primitive Marcan fragment itself, we find the same consistent and unvarying witness to the disappearance of the body. If the situation had been the other way round; if we had been asked to believe something which was *denied* by every solitary manuscript which has survived the centuries, how solid and unanswerable would that cumulative and absolutely unanimous denial appear! What play could be made by the dialectician with the fact that not the smallest chink or loophole had been left for doubt. Surely (it would be contended), the real truth must have blundered somewhere to the light. Yet in all the varied literature from that far-off time, written under different skies, by men of varying temperaments, possessed by obviously divergent theories of the true course of those memorable events, there has come down to us no hint or suggestion that the facts about the grave were other than those substantially recorded in the Gospel according to St. Mark. However disconcerting the fact may be, the literary verdict is unanimous and must at least be given its due weight by the impartial mind.

But there is something far more arresting and significant than even this unanimous literary witness, and I do not see how even the most confident of modern critics can view it steadily and consistently without experiencing a feeling of profound disquiet and unrest. I mean the extraordinary silence of antiquity concerning the later history of the grave of Jesus.

It is strange—this absolutely unbroken silence concerning a spot which must have been a very sacred place to thousands of people outside the circle of the Christian believers themselves. If the disciples were deceived in this matter, or if the intensity of their faith in the Appearances led them to ignore or to attach no importance to the condition of the grave, what of the preponderant mass of the Jewish public outside? Did no one regard with reverence the sepulchre which held the mortal remains of the greatest Teacher that Israel had seen since the prophetic days? Had Joseph of Arimathea and Nicodemus no counterpart among all the toiling multitudes who crowded round the boats on the shores of Galilee and filled Capernaum and Cana and Nazareth with tumultuous throngs? Surely for every man or woman who came under the magnetic influence of the disciples there must have been a hundred who had no illusions concerning the grave, but were filled with profound grief and sorrow by the untimely death of Christ.

Yet we can search in vain for any sign or hint or whisper that during those first four crucial years when the Christians were teaching their strange doctrine within the walls of Jerusalem there was a stream of pilgrims to that silent grotto beyond the gate. We catch no echo of any controversy between the many who knew the real facts and the deluded few who taught and presumably believed otherwise. Why did the least believable of all the cults of Christianity survive and leave no traces of the one rational and divergent form which, according to all reasonable expectation, ought to have overmastered it and triumphed in its stead?

Or take the same central problem from another and slightly different point of view. Let the reader sit down and in the quiet of his own study ponder one very simple but searching question. Why was it that *Jerusalem* became the centre and focus of this mad unreason which in the coming years was to spread itself outwards to the uttermost limits of the Roman world? Why Jerusalem in preference to Capernaum, or even Nazareth itself? There are a hundred reasons why so demonstrably fragile a myth as the belief in the physical resurrection of Jesus ought to have flourished in the congenial soil of Galilee and to have withered within the precincts of the real grave.

Jerusalem was always hostile and unsympathetic to the genius of Christ; Galilee was His home. Those who loved Him best and must have mourned Him most came from that smiling province. No one seriously doubts that within fourteen days of the Crucifixion Peter and Andrew and some others of the Apostolic band stood upon the shores of that inland sea and felt the call of their ancient and honourable trade. Granted that a vision came to one of them and perhaps to all. But why did not this mystic church of believers spring into being and strike its deepest and most central roots in Galilee, the spiritual home of Jesus, a place impregnated with His personality and teaching? Why did everybody who caught the infection of this spring madness gravitate to Jerusalem as steel to a magnet? Why should so irrational a doctrine flourish most readily and take its implacable stand in the veritable presence and vicinity of that which it denied?

There is only one answer to all these questions which satisfies alike the unanimous literary witness and the collateral requirements of historical circumstance. It lies in the assumption that the story of the women's visit to the grave—as given in all its primitive and naked simplicity in the Marcan fragment—is the true story. It was told, not because it had any particular apologetic value—for as an apologetic it can be riddled with criticism—but because things fell out that way. In other words, it was a fact of history.

*   *   *   *   *

Now immediately we begin to think of this story about the women, not as a legend of comparatively late growth, but as historic fact, we begin to discern certain characteristics of the Marcan version which stamp it very noticeably with the marks and evidences of truth.

Consider first the identity of the women who are reported to have visited the tomb. It would have been a very strange thing if *nobody* had gone to pay a last tribute to a friend so noble and so lovable as Christ. It would have been stranger still if the band of mourners had not been predominantly women. Yet it would have been the strangest thing of all if they had not been these particular women. They fit the circumstances as the hand fits the glove.

After all, Jesus was their man and they were His women. If we had been told that it was Claudia Procula, or Lazarus, or even Nicodemus who paid the clandestine visit to the grave we should, I think, in the absence of strong corroborative evidence, be justified in harbouring a doubt. But who were more likely to attempt this last poignant service to the dead leader than the mothers of His men and the woman whose life His influence had utterly transfigured? When, therefore, Professor Schmiedel would have us believe that the story about the women is unhistorical and was probably circulated for the first time towards the close of the Apostolic Age, I am bound to say quite frankly that I do not believe him. And I base that conclusion on something far greater than any fact which he adduces—the mighty and unchanging instincts of the human heart, especially the feminine heart. Regarded as legend this story denies the most probable thing in the whole history. It is precisely when we regard it as fact that we find it to be firmly based upon the solid and enduring foundations of human experience.

Now this sense of a certain vital trueness when regarded as fact, and a certain unreality when regarded as fiction, becomes even more pronounced when we look more closely into the details of the story. St. Mark says that after their strange encounter at the tomb the women ran away, and the language which he uses suggests that they did so in a state of some confusion and alarm. His words are: 'They went out, and fled from the tomb; for trembling and astonishment had come upon them.' He adds further the very significant words: 'They said nothing to anyone; for they were afraid. . . .'

We do not know what the writer of St. Mark originally set down as the closing words of this sentence, for the famous fragment breaks off abruptly at this point. But whatever the conclusion may have been, the sense of the main passage is clear. The women, after witnessing the burial on Friday afternoon, decided to pay their last act of respect and love to Jesus on Sunday morning. It was quite obviously a clandestine visit, partly no doubt because the garden was private property, but chiefly because they feared the Priests. Peter's angry denial in the courtyard of the High Priest's house shows that it was a dangerous thing, during those hours when deadly passions were let loose, to be associated even distantly, with the party of the Nazarene.

They set out according to a prearranged plan shortly before dawn, when comparatively few people would be about and when, according to their view, the garden would

almost certainly be deserted. Clearly they had no inkling or
expectation of anything abnormal. Their sole preoccupation was with the stone which they knew to be heavy and the
removal of which might be beyond their strength. Looking
to the right and to the left lest their errand should be
detected, they softly approached the tomb. A few moments
later they were fleeing through the entrance of the garden
into the open road.

Such in its broad outlines is the Marcan account of what
happened. It reads like a transcript from real life. Its very
defects as a legend are the strongest proof of its actuality.
The terror of the women, their failure to make more than a
momentary inspection of the tomb, their precipitate retreat
and reported silence—all these are strange ingredients in a
story told with apologetic intent thirty years later or indeed
at any time after the event. Regarded as fact they are like a
breeze of truth blowing across the landscape on that
historic morning.

*   *   *   *   *

Two facts, therefore, seem to stand out clearly as belonging to the historic certainties in this matter. First, that
certain women of the party of Jesus really did go to the
tomb in the early hours of Sunday morning; second, that a
few moments later they fled from the garden in a state of
some excitement and alarm. Now it seems to me that, quite
apart from what we are told in the Marcan fragment, we
should be compelled to infer that the women met someone
at the tomb. Their shaken nerve and their precipitate retreat
demands it. Had the garden been deserted, had they come
merely to an empty cave (or even to a closed one) they might
have been halted in perplexity, but they would hardly have
run away. It requires a presence to produce that sense of
instant confusion and precipitate departure. And the
curious thing is that it seems to demand a human presence.
I will ask the reader particularly to ponder that point.

In the nature of things we do not and cannot know how a
normal human being would act if it were possible for him or

her to be confronted suddenly by an authentic visitant from another world. It is perhaps almost idle to inquire. I cannot help feeling, however, that if the vision produced the kind of impression which we associate with an 'angel' the result would not be to induce terror, but rather a slowly dawning wonder, a consciousness of the nearness of great and sacred things. If the visitor possessed also the power of speech there would be something in the tone to allay fear and to compel attention. It is not so easy after all to think of such a vision striking terror into the hearts of pious women.

But to come suddenly and unexpectedly upon another person, without warning of any kind, in the interior of a rather dark cave at dawn, is a very different matter. The situation is saturated with terrifying possibilities. It provides precisely that element of mental and moral shock which the Marcan account of this episode so clearly demands. It must never be forgotten that on any reading of the affair this visit to the tomb was in the strictest sense hazardous and risky. It is not by accident or apologetic design that dawn was chosen by these faithful and heroic friends of Christ. It was the one golden and fleeting moment of opportunity. Every minute that passed after the sun had risen increased their peril. They were clearly committing a trespass in entering the garden at all, and they knew it. That, I take it, is the meaning of the phrase: 'They feared lest any man should see them.' It is certainly a fundamental element in the psychological atmosphere of St. Mark.

*   *   *   *   *

Thus we come face to face with a very interesting fact. Test it where we will, this story has the peculiar and authentic ring of truth. It does not read like a story invented many years afterwards to lend colour and support to the Christian theory of the Resurrection. It looks far more like an original recollection of an actual event. And yet, even when we have said this, I doubt if we shall have realized how near this famous old fragment comes to what Dr. Bartlet calls the 'sheer historic facts'. Indeed, I do not think that we shall ever reach a full understanding of the Resurrection problem until we are prepared to recognize that the story of the women's adventure, as told in this very early narrative, is not only the true story in the sense that the women actually went, and that they fled on discovering another person in the tomb, but true also in the far deeper and more important sense, that the place they visited really was the *original grave of Christ*.

Let the reader go to some quiet place apart and think out that issue to its logical conclusion. Let him recall first that all the hypotheses which have come down to us from a remote antiquity, purporting to explain the resurrection phenomena, take as their basic assumption the physical vacancy of the real tomb.

This is the more noteworthy because criticism on strictly rational grounds was not wanting even in the earliest days of Christianity. Every conceivable taunt and imputation which it was possible to hurl at the disciples and their cause is reflected in the literature. We read at great length, for example, of the charge that Jesus was born of fornication; that the disciples threatened to set the Temple on fire; that Joseph of Arimathea could not be found when he was wanted; that the women were seen at the tomb as early as midnight; that the body was discovered by Pilate in a neighbouring well. All these and many other innuendoes can be found in the apocryphal literature. Yet when we do come at last upon indubitable snatches of controversy about the real issue we find—not, as we should have expected, that the vacancy of the grave was stoutly and categorically denied, but that the disciples were accused of having abducted the body. It is strange, this failure of the keenest intellects in Judea to put their finger upon the one solid and unanswerable argument that it had never been disturbed!

It is strange, too, that no one ever thought of the simple expedient of confronting the disciples, and especially the women, with the individual who, beyond all question, knew what had taken place. *For there was a witness in the garden that morning*.

By the very irony of circumstances, on the day that

173

brought the women to the tomb, at the identical hour of their visit (viz. shortly after dawn), and in the precise spot which from the standpoint of the hypothesis is of supreme importance, a young man was working. He not only saw the women approach and run away, but (we are told) he recognized their mistake and tried to point out to them where the real tomb lay. He was, therefore, a completely detached and independent observer of the whole episode.

Having regard to the exceptionally early hour at which this encounter took place, it is reasonable to suppose that this young man must have been either the official gardener or custodian of the place or a workman preparing the tomb for an imminent interment. In either event we reach a situation profoundly and even ludicrously destructive of the women's case. If the young man whom they surprised at the tomb was the gardener, he was there to be questioned at any time, and to give the true version of what had taken place. It can hardly be contended that he would not remember encountering three agitated women at such an unusual hour and bent upon such an exceptional mission. If he was a workman, preparing the grave for an interment, then some Jewish citizen must actually have been buried in the mistaken tomb within a few hours.

Thus, there was the young man himself to whom appeal could be made; there were the friends, relatives and mourners of the deceased person, who had only too sorrowful an occasion to know that the latter was buried within a few yards of the notorious Nazarene! Can we imagine, with all this conclusive evidence available, that the personal enemies of the disciples (and they were many) would never have sought it out?

Surely we cannot, and in that simple reply, it seems to me, lies the dismissal of the theory of the women's mistake. For whether they told their story within the first seven minutes or, as Dr. Lake believes, at the end of the first few weeks, the result must have been the same. Think of those four years of persistent propaganda and steadily deepening conviction and success. Think of the weekly discussions and disputations in the synagogues. Think of the innumerable private controversies as to whether this Jesus was the Messiah or whether He was not. Think of the highly placed Sadducees who were prepared to go to almost any length to discredit and overthrow the cause. Think of the opposition suddenly being reinforced by the logical and relentless mind of Saul.

Think of all these admittedly historic things and then reflect that the evidence which could have pricked the bubble was to be obtained for the asking by merely walking a distance no greater than that from Hyde Park Corner to the Marble Arch. Think of another matter, too. What an impetus such inquiries would have given to that contemporary veneration of the *real* resting-place of Jesus, of which, as we have seen, there is not a trace!

Personally, I am convinced that no body of men or women could persistently and successfully have preached in Jerusalem a doctrine involving the vacancy of that tomb, without the grave itself being physically vacant. The facts were too recent; the tomb too close to that seething centre of oriental life. Not all the make-believe in the world could have purchased the utter silence of antiquity or given to the records their impressive unanimity. Only the truth, in all its unavoidable simplicity, could have achieved that.

*   *   *   *   *

I would have the reader mark also one curious but very suggestive detail of the narrative, to which, for various reasons, attention has not hitherto been drawn. It concerns the young man whom, according to St. Mark, the women surprised in occupation of the tomb. This is a matter which will bear close and attentive study.

St. Mark does not leave us in doubt whether the young man was standing close to the tomb or working some little distance away from it. He tells us explicitly that on 'entering into the tomb', the women found him '*sitting* on the right side'. Thus his presence remained undisclosed until that one terrifying moment when the women were on the point of entering the cave. Hence clearly their consternation and precipitate departure. Had this young man been the ordinary gardener of the place, working in the open and in full view of those who approached, the women would surely never have reached the door of the tomb at all. Most probably they would have halted a short distance away and, upon deciding to retire, would have done so discreetly and unobtrusively. But this, of course, is not the Marcan picture at all. According to our document the shock came at the very entrance to the cave, where, in the nature of things, they were least prepared for it.

If, therefore, this element of sudden surprise is essential to the Marcan picture, what are we to make of the strange occupation of the visitor? The interior of a dark and untenanted cave at dawn is a very strange resting-place for a workman who had a serious job in hand. If he was the gardener, what was he doing inside the tomb at all, when he could have rested in so much greater comfort in the fresh, cool air outside? Why the need of rest in a sepulchral and unhealthy atmosphere when dawn had only just broken? There does not seem to be any visible reason for a normal human being occupying a death chamber at such an unusual hour unless he had come expressly for the purpose, and had some very real and definite interest in the tomb.

And it is of course precisely that intense interest in the contents of this particular grave which can explain adequately why a young man who had just run all the way from Jerusalem could be discovered a few minutes later 'sitting in the tomb'. There must have been something peculiarly provocative of thought in the spectacle of that vacant ledge, especially if, as two of our Gospels assert, the grave-clothes were still there. We can imagine him sitting down to ponder what this strange phenomenon might mean until a few moments later he was disturbed by footfalls and whispering voices without. For a brief moment the figure of a young woman darkened the door and was gone, and running out he saw three agitated women fleeing in alarm. He called after them a message which either they did not hear, or were too unnerved and frightened to heed. This is only a small detail very likely to be overlooked by a fabricator with his mind intent upon an angel, but deeply impressive when regarded as an integral part of the original facts.

*   *   *   *   *

But there is another, and a very strong reason, for believing that the place the women visited could not have been other than the original tomb of Christ. It must be obvious to anyone who gives this matter a moment's thought that Mary Magdalene and her friends must have told their story at the earliest possible moment consistent with their own safety and that of the disciples. To suppose that three women (two of them already well advanced in middle age) could go through an unnerving experience like that—an experience calculated to leave an indelible mark upon their minds—and to say nothing about it even to their closest friends, is absurd. Dr. Lake has pleaded, however, for a delay of about three weeks on the ground that the disciples were not in Jerusalem. Let us grant that provisionally, but beyond the date of the disciples' return no reasonable person can be constrained to go. It is certain that this essential reunion could not have been effected later than the Feast of Weeks, when it is commonly agreed that the whole party was again in Jerusalem. The disciples were therefore in possession of the story before the vital date of Pentecost. If the women had not told their story by then, surely nothing would have extracted it from them.

Now it is here that we begin to meet a fact of very high historical significance, for it is clear that *the disciples did not make use of the story* as evidence of the Resurrection. There is not a word about the women's experience in the famous Whitsuntide sermons which launched the Christian movement upon its historic course. We catch no hint of its being employed in the other speeches recorded in the Acts. And, as though to clinch the matter, there is a curious and suggestive silence throughout the Missionary Epistles, including St. Paul's famous letter to the Corinthians, where, if anywhere, we should have expected to find it. In all this varied literature and correspondence there is a neglect of the

177

women's evidence which wears almost the aspect of a suppression. Yet St. Luke, who took no inconsiderable part in the work of the Early Church, and who was for long months the intimate companion of St. Paul, evidently knew the story, since he related it in his own Gospel. So also did St. Mark, who similarly spent some time with St. Paul.

What was the explanation of this very pointed and obvious suppression of a phase of the Easter experiences which was to become later one of the most treasured of Christian memories? Why was it that when the great series of written lives of Jesus began to appear, embodying those traditions which through long usage had engraved themselves imperishably upon the recollections of the Church, we find this story about the women embedded deeply and inextricably at the centre and heart of the whole matter? There *is* an explanation big enough to satisfy this and the other varied aspects of this many-sided problem.

Let us go back to the early hours of that memorable Easter. As everyone who has attentively studied the Gospels knows, there are strong reasons for thinking that the message which Mary Magdalene brought back to the city shortly after dawn was not to the effect that Jesus had risen, but that for some unexplained reason *the body had been removed*. This is the clear testimony of the record which tells us what one of the women actually said within a few minutes of the discovery.

We must picture these three women, after their terrifying experience at the grave, running away from that place of dread as hard as they could towards the open road. Their ages were dissimilar. Mary Magdalene was a young woman; the two others were the mothers of grown men. Arrived in the public highway it must have become clear that someone ought to run ahead and inform the disciples. Mary Magdalene, as the youngest and most agile of the party, would almost certainly volunteer, leaving the older women to follow at their own pace. A few moments later we read of a breathless and obviously distressed girl knocking at the door of a certain house in Jerusalem and delivering her historic message: 'They have taken away the Lord

178

out of the tomb and we know not where they have laid him.'

Such was the message, in all its primitive despair and
urgency, which Mary Magdalene brought to the disciples
Peter and John. Meanwhile I think it is very probable that
the two older women, returning home as fast as they could,
related to their friends a rather fuller account of what had
occurred, in which prominence was given to the unexpected
visitor to the grave. Indeed, it is not unlikely that already the
thought that the young man was an angel may have begun
to take shape in their minds. This would account for the very
definite statement in the Emmaus document preserved by
St. Luke:

'Moreover certain women of our company amazed us, having
been early at the tomb; and when they found not his body, they
came, saying, that they had also seen a vision of angels, which said
that he was alive.'

So the early hours of the morning passed in a welter of
excitement and confused questionings as to what the events
in the garden might mean.

If matters had ended here the course of history might have
been changed, for there can be no doubt that when the disciples were at last convinced that the Lord had risen, the
women's testimony would have been produced in evidence;
the identity of the young man would have been raised, and
the whole question of the encounter at the tomb would
have become a matter of public discussion. But, as I read
the situation, events took a very different and far more
formidable course. Before the sun had risen far in the
eastern sky a strange, but very definite rumour began to
circulate through the crowded streets and bazaars of the
city. It came, not from irresponsible sources, but from
members of the Temple Guard. The details were circumstantial, and the story was that the disciples had stolen the
body of the Nazarene.

The blow fell, in all its bitter injustice and startling
suddenness, upon a party not yet fully reassembled after the
hurried flight of Thursday night. It menaced the safety of
everyone who was known, even distantly, to have had con-

nections with the Nazarene. Late that evening the disciples found it expedient to meet under conditions of great secrecy behind barred doors. That night also, according to ancient tradition, the Appearances, those strange projections from the world of spirit into the world of sense, began.

Confusing as these events must have seemed at the time to those who passed through them, one fact is clear. The physical vacancy of the tomb itself was not in doubt. Immediately we recognize this we begin to get real light upon the historical reasons for the suppression of the women's story.

The women's experience was not used as evidence at any period during the early Jewish-Christian controversy for two very simple but sufficient reasons. In the first place it proved nothing which was not already conceded by the other side. The only fact which the story could establish was that, at about six o'clock on Sunday morning, the body of Jesus was no longer in the place where Joseph had laid it. But who wanted to prove something which was not only common knowledge, but which was being made the basis of a very serious charge against the disciples themselves?

Secondly, the story possessed the grave weakness of admitting that certain members of the Christian party had actually been in the neighbourhood of the tomb under conditions of some secrecy and at a suspiciously early hour on the morning in question. This was a very damaging admission to make in the peculiar circumstances in which the disciples found themselves. In all ages the essence of a good defence against a serious charge has been to prove an alibi. If a man is accused of committing a murder in Lincoln's Inn Fields and he can show proof that at the time the deed was committed he was asleep in his bed at Notting Hill, he will probably be acquitted. If, however, he admits in cross-examination that he really was out that night, that he was in the neighbourhood of Lincoln's Inn Fields shortly after the time of the murder, and was actually looking for the deceased man, he will increase the difficulties of his counsel tenfold.

Now that, as I understand it, was precisely the situation

as regards the followers of Jesus. They were being charged publicly with having abducted the body. It was a very difficult charge to refute even if they had been free to come out into the open, but we have reasons for believing that they were in hiding, meeting in clandestine fashion behind closed doors. What would it have meant to that broken little remnant of Christ's party to have admitted openly that the women had been at the tomb! What a handle it would have given to their opponents to have been able to say that, on their own confession, the Christians had been hanging about the garden at dawn!

Anyone who looks at this matter impartially will see that during that never-to-be-forgotten week, when no one knew what fresh dangers and humiliations were in store for them, the whole tendency would be to say as little as possible about the abortive visit to the grave. And, surprising though it may seem, this reluctance on the part of the early Christians to give prominence to the women's testimony did unquestionably persist through early Christian times.

It is impossible to read through the early chapters of the Acts with their very detailed accounts of the primitive preaching without being impressed by the singular absence of contention regarding the tomb. If it had ever seriously been doubted that the body was missing, the adventure of the women and what it implied must have been thrust by the implacable force of events into the very foreground of the Christian dialectic. It would have overshadowed every other consideration, for until that was settled nothing fundamental to the Christian thesis stood.

But the disciples were obviously spared this interminable and fruitless wrangle. The facts were so well known that the campaign they undertook could positively be conducted with greater success in Jerusalem, where the abandoned tomb lay, than in any other place in the world. It was this which enabled them to concentrate (as the Acts clearly show that they did) upon the two vital contentions which ultimately rent Judaism asunder, viz. that Jesus was the promised Messiah, and that He had been raised by the direct hand of God. They could surely never have reached this advanced stage of the discussion so early, if the physical vacancy of the tomb had not been common ground.

*   *   *   *   *

Thus we can see how, as a matter of historic fact, the adventure of the women at the grave did sink into comparative oblivion beside the much vaster and more vital issues which events determined. Its memory was cherished personally by the women themselves, for they alone had the honour of originating a very human service to their Master at a time of great danger and uncertainty. It was known to the disciples themselves. In quieter and more settled times it was doubtless included in the instructions of the Church. And out of that widespread dissemination of the story throughout the Christian churches of Europe and Asia arose all those divergent and developed accounts of which St. Luke and St. Matthew's versions are typical.

Thus the young man at the grave, who really was a young man in the original story, became in course of time the great angel of St. Matthew, and the two mighty and dazzling celestial visitants of St. Luke. Thus, too, the rolling away of the stone, the true history of which was known only to the priests, became the subject of numerous conjectures, some saying that it rolled away of itself, others that the angels moved it. But behind all these secondary versions stood the simple and historic facts.

It is when we recognize this clearly that we begin to understand something of the meaning and significance of that wonderful document which throughout these pages I have described as the Marcan fragment. Many years later, when the hopes of an immediate return of Christ were fading, and the Church was settling down to its historic work, the need was felt for some connected record of the outstanding events of life and death of Jesus. The earliest extant history of that kind is the famous fragment of St. Mark. If the writer was John Mark, he was singularly fitted for telling that story, especially the closing chapters. He was a Jerusalemite who as a youth lived through those stormy and tempestuous days. That he had access to first-

hand information about the closing week is obvious from
the minuteness, the almost startling sharpness and fidelity
of his detail. No one but a writer in close touch with the
facts could have given us that unforgettable moonlight
picture of the Garden of Gethsemane. I submit, too, that
there are touches in his description of the women's adventure which suggest a similar authentic source.

For some reason St. Mark believed that Jesus had not only
predicted His own death, but His resurrection also. He
believed, too, that shortly before His death, on the way to
Gethsemane, Our Lord reiterated that solemn warning.
With these conceptions in his mind and with the first-hand
information which reached him from other sources, he
pieced together and built up one of the most graphic pieces
of description in all literature. It stands out above its
fellows by its sheer objectivity, the crystalline quality of its
clarity.

He describes the vigil in the garden and the midnight
arrest in words which only too plainly rest upon fact. He
gives us a really intelligible account of the trial before
Caiaphas and the abasement of Peter. He describes the
Roman trial, the journey to Calvary, and the Crucifixion,
in language so simple and yet so poignant that as Mr.
Chesterton has truly said the reader feels as though rocks
had been rolled over him.

He describes how, just as the awful tragedy was coming to
its culmination, Joseph of Arimathea went to Pilate for permission to bury the body, and obtained it. He tells how the
stricken and sorrowing women followed in Joseph's trail,
and beheld where the body was laid; and how, as the sun
went down upon that awful afternoon, the stone was hurriedly but reverently placed across the mouth of the cave.
He also explains how, having bought spices during the
week-end, the women arose early on Sunday morning
and came to the tomb at dawn.

*   *   *   *   *

Now in considering what follows we must never allow
ourselves to forget that St. Mark was probably putting the

story of the Easter experiences into writing for the first time and for certain reasons the original facts differed from what was being currently taught over wide areas of the Christian Church.

The very fact that such slight prominence was given to the women's experience in the public preaching of the original apostles left the door open for the widest diversity of belief as to what really happened at the grave. In some circles it was believed and taught that an angel descended and spoke to the women; in others that there were two angels. The widespread and divergent character of these beliefs is plainly shown in the first and third Gospels. St. Matthew and St. Luke did not *create* these versions. They doubtless recorded faithfully what had long been believed and taught in widely separated centres of the Church's work.

In writing the history of these events, therefore, St. Mark approached a difficult and delicate task. Since he himself was a mere youth at the time of the Crucifixion he was one of the few survivors of the Primitive Church. He had lived through that troubled week in Jerusalem, and knew the essence of the matter as it was known to the original disciples. But he could not escape the fact that the true story told in all its bluntness and simplicity would come with a strangely chilling effect to many who had been nurtured upon the more glowing and supernatural accounts.

To those who had been brought up in the belief that the women had encountered an angel at the tomb, it must have seemed a very extraordinary thing that they did not immediately proclaim the Resurrection and bring all Jerusalem to the garden to witness its result. It was the old problem of the 'seven-weeks' gap'.

But St. Mark knew the facts, and anticipating that question he wrote a sentence which either he never completed or the end of which has been lost:

'They said nothing to anyone; for they were afraid. . . .'

Much has been written with the intent to show that St. Mark meant by these words that the women maintained an absolute silence. It is admitted that it was a very unnatural

184

thing for them to do, but there the words are, and in the submission of certain critics they admit of no other meaning.

I venture to suggest that they admit of a far simpler and more natural explanation, and in support of that contention I will call no less a witness than the writer of the Marcan fragment itself.

It so happens that in chapter i, verse 44, of St. Mark's Gospel there is a sentence so similar in construction and purport to the one which we are now considering as to constitute a very striking parallel. Jesus had just healed a leper of his disease. He was very anxious that news of this work of healing should not get about. St. Mark says that He strictly charged him and straightway sent him out and saith unto him: 'See thou say nothing to any man. . . .' Note carefully the close resemblance between the two sentences: 'See thou say nothing to any man'—'They said nothing to anyone.' Both contain the same unqualified word: 'nothing'. Both come from the same pen. Let us suppose that St. Mark's Gospel had ended abruptly at this point. Should we be justified in assuming that the silence was to be regarded as unconditional? Volumes could be written to prove that we should. In strict logic, and detached from their context, the words can bear no other meaning. Yet, *we should be wrong*, for here is the completed sentence as St. Mark wrote it:

'And [Jesus] saith unto him, See thou say nothing to any man: but go thy way, shew thyself to the priest, and offer for thy cleansing the things which Moses commanded, for a testimony unto them.'

Immediately we get the full thought of the writer before us, it is obvious that he uses the words: 'See thou say nothing to any man' in the sense: 'Do not publish this abroad. Keep it to yourself and to those intimately concerned.' For he follows on with what would otherwise be a direct negative of the original injunction.

With all deference to Prof. Kirsopp Lake, the Rev. P. Gardner-Smith, and those critics who affirm that St. Mark implied the absolute and unconditional silence of the women, I am convinced they are wrong and that the words will not bear the extreme meaning which it is sought to extract from them. The phrase as used by St. Mark in relation to the women's adventure is palpably an *anticipation of a question* which would spring to the mind of every reader to whom this newly written biography would come as a deeply interesting thing. Remember that the Matthean and Lucan documents were as yet unpublished. People would say: 'If the women discovered the Resurrection at such an early hour on Sunday morning, why was not all Jerusalem aroused and summoned to witness the result?' St. Mark's reply to this is exact and strictly historical: 'They said nothing to anyone; for they were afraid. . . .'

Thus to the long line of witnesses whose testimony we have been considering in these pages—of Simon the fisherman who stood in the forefront of the original battle in Jerusalem; of the writers of St. Luke, St. Matthew and St. John; of James the Just; of Saul of Tarsus; of the authors or editors of the apocryphal gospels of Peter and Nicodemus; even of the golal or great stone itself—we have finally to add the writer of the most famous fragment in all literature, the broken sentence of St. Mark.

Chapter XV

THE SERVANT OF THE PRIEST

Who was the young man who, if this interpretation be the true one, anticipated the women and shared with them the earliest experiences of that memorable morning? We shall probably never know, for if St. Mark withheld his name it must have been for very good and sufficient reasons. But there is one thought in that connection which I venture to think will bear profound and repeated study.

If the reader will take the last eight verses of St. Mark's Gospel (chapter xvi, verses 1 to 8) and will study them carefully, remembering that they represent probably the earliest written account of these events, he will, I think, be pulled up very sharply by one fact—the absence of any hint or suggestion as to how the stone itself came to be moved. An impenetrable curtain descends abruptly at the conclusion of the burial on Friday afternoon and does not rise again until dawn on Sunday, when the stone has already been removed. Why was this? Did the Church, as late as A.D. 58, know nothing of what happened during that critical period, or was St. Mark writing under the pressure of some intense reserve?

The point is worth pondering because the same curious reluctance to deal with the physical cause of the movement of the stone comes out very strikingly in the parallel passages from St. Luke and St. John. St. Luke says:

'But on the first day of the week, at early dawn, they [the women] came unto the tomb, bringing the spices which they had prepared. And they found the stone rolled away from the tomb. And they entered in, and found not the body of the Lord Jesus.'

187

St. John's version is no less peculiar and arresting:

'The first day of the week cometh Mary Magdalene early, while it was yet dark, unto the tomb, and seeth the stone taken away from the tomb. She runneth, therefore . . .' etc.

In each case the women arrive to find the stone already rolled away, yet with no hint from the writers as to how this came about. It is only when we turn to St. Matthew's Gospel that we read of a great angel descending and removing the stone.

Now the peculiar and significant thing is this. We can search the apocryphal writings through and through, and we shall nowhere find even the remotest suggestion that the Lord Himself broke the barriers of His own prison. We are told that the stone 'rolled away of itself', or that supernatural beings descended and moved it. But nowhere is the obvious miracle recorded that Jesus Himself threw down the physical defences of the grave.

Why did nobody ever say that the Lord Himself, of His own power and might, thrust aside the stone and achieved release from the cave? Why does every document which discusses this question assume that the stone was moved *from without*—either by an angel or by means of invisible power?

I suggest that we are here in the presence of a deep and far-reaching historical fact—a fact which laid its compulsion upon everyone and diverted ultimately the very course of tradition. The moving of the stone was never ascribed to the power of the risen Lord Himself because there were men in Jerusalem who knew the real facts concerning what happened during those dark hours which preceded the dawn on Sunday. Those facts precluded the hypothesis being truthfully advanced, and for evidence of that we must turn yet again to that ancient and curiously archaic story of the guard.

I have already given reason for believing that in the original and true version of this story the priests went to Pilate, late on Saturday afternoon or early evening, in the hope of arranging with him for the policing of the grave— a precaution very desirable in view of the unpredictable attitude of the populace when the restraint of the Sabbath observance was removed. Pilate refused their request, as St. Matthew's version clearly shows, and the priests had no alternative but to fall back upon the Temple Guard for this necessary duty.

Now there are two very good reasons for thinking that St. Matthew's version of this incident, while not perhaps the original and primitive form of the story, is so near to that original as to constitute a valuable basis of historical study. In the first place it is by far the earliest form in which the story has come down to us. Secondly, it is entirely free from those illogicalities which crept into it in a later age.

This fact is strikingly demonstrated in the language of the guarantee which the priests are reported to have given to the members of the guard: 'If this come to the governor's ears, we will persuade him, and rid you of care.' So long as the guard is thought of as a Roman detachment, set by Pilate himself under the command of a centurion (as in the later and derivative accounts it was represented to have been), this guarantee will seem utterly illogical and absurd. It was perfectly well known that the penalty for sleeping at the post of duty was death, and neither Annas, nor Caiaphas, nor any member of the Jewish camarilla had the power to protect a single Roman soldier from the wrath of Rome.

But Caiaphas, as the Acting High Priest and the supreme arbiter of the civil destinies of Judea, did unquestionably possess the power to protect a member of his own entourage, acting under orders, in the very unlikely event of the Procurator interesting himself in a matter which he had expressly deposited in Jewish hands. The very words: '*If* this come to the governor's ears,' show how remote this contingency was felt to be. I mention the point here because a great deal of thoughtless and superficial criticism has been directed against a feature of the story which did not and could not have formed part of the primitive account.

But there is a far deeper and more suggestive bit of evidence for the historicity of the story embedded in the documents. It lies in the last three words of the explanation attributed to the priests: 'the disciples stole him away *while we slept*.'

What are these three words doing in a pro-Christian document, circulating widely throughout Palestine, if they do not represent something very real and actual in the original charge? Let us grant that the story of a guard at the tomb had a certain apologetic value to the early Christians, since it made it more difficult for unbiased persons to believe in the physical abduction of the body. But the essence of this defence was that the guard should keep awake. *A guard which slept was of no use to the Christians*, and was futile and dangerous as an apologetic. Why, then, did this strange reference to the sleeping of the guard become embedded, not only in the wording of the charge itself, but also in the Christian version of what happened?

I submit that the awkward and peculiar nature of the circumstances left no alternative to the priests, for the whole truth they dared not tell. It may indeed be that the guard really did fall asleep, from sheer exhaustion, during some part of that memorable night. When we remember that these men were probably drawn at short notice from the Temple police who had been on practically continuous duty since the arrest on the previous Thursday, this is by no means improbable. The policing of a deserted garden outside the city wall, throughout the dark hours of an April night, after a prolonged spell of exhausting duty elsewhere, may well have been monotonous and devoid of interest. There were probably no signs of nocturnal visitors, and, as the long hours dragged wearily by, need we be surprised if sleep overcame them?

Since the records have perished, the truth concerning that matter will probably never be disclosed. But there is one hint in an obscure and long-forgotten document which I am bound to confess comes to me personally with peculiar weight. It is in that strange old fragment, of which only a few sentences survive—the Gospel of the Hebrews. There is a passage in that document which describes how Jesus, after His resurrection, appeared to His brother James. I will give it in full:

'Now the Lord, when he had given the linen cloth unto the servant of the priest, went unto James and appeared to him (for James had sworn that he would not eat bread from that hour wherein he had drunk the Lord's cup until he should see him risen again from among them that sleep),' and again after a little: 'Bring ye, saith the Lord, a table and bread' and immediately it is added: 'He took bread and blessed and brake and gave it unto James the Just and said unto him: My brother, eat thy bread, for the Son of Man is risen from among them that sleep.'

What is it about this famous passage which arrests and challenges our thought? Primarily, of course, that the central fact of which it speaks is attested independently by two of the weightiest historical considerations in the world. First, it is undeniable that, despite his earlier and unfeigned hostility, James, the brother of Jesus, did go over to the Church and that, upon the authority of Josephus, he perished violently on its behalf. Second, there is the authentic voice of Paul, calling to us, as it were, across the centuries with a certain quiet insistence: 'He appeared unto James.' The agreement of two such witnesses lends to this passage an authority almost exclusively its own.

What, then, are we to make of that curious and significant sentence which describes Jesus as giving 'the linen cloth to the servant of the priest'? Is this a complete invention, a flight of fancy, or are we here right back in some vaguely remembered detail of the original night? I will venture to warn the reader not to return too hasty an answer.

If there be one thing in the New Testament which threatens to emerge unchallenged from the present religious and intellectual turmoil it is the real and objective character of the Appearances. This phenomenon could not have been the product of pure imagination. Rather does it seem to call for some undiscovered but externally exerted force. The simplest explanation, of course, is that the manifestations occurred where Jesus Himself was. There are signs in the Gospels that there may have been difficulties of a real and strictly scientific kind in establishing communication between what (for want of a more exact phrase) we must call the world of spirit and the world of sense. There is a certain quality in the *daylight* Appearances which suggests that recognition was occasionally difficult, or, as a modern physicist would put it, the visibility was poor.

But such parallels as we possess seem to indicate that darkness is favourable to certain delicate forms of transmission and reception. Do not even our wireless signals fade and recover as the twilight passes into the night?

I have an impression, not solely dependent upon this isolated passage in the Gospel of the Hebrews, that as dawn approached in that quiet garden, something happened which caused one of the watchers hurriedly to awaken his companions and to proceed to a closer inspection of the tomb. It may have been only the stirring of the trees, or the clanging of a gate in the night breeze. It may have been something more definite and disquieting, such as that which later shook and utterly humbled the proud and relentless spirit of St. Paul. 'He appeared to Cephas . . . then to the twelve . . . he appeared to James . . . last of all, as unto one born out of due time, he appeared to me.' Did He appear also in the first instance to 'the servant of the priest'?

If that were so, then we should indeed have stumbled, almost unconsciously, upon the true answer to one of the profoundest questions which has engaged the thought of the Church from the time of the Early Fathers to our own—viz. why it was that, despite the wavering of tradition concerning the locality of the Appearances, the disciples were so immovably convinced that the Resurrection itself took place in the early hours of Sunday morning.

There may be, and, as the writer thinks, there certainly is, a deep and profoundly historical basis for that much disputed sentence in the Apostles' Creed—'The *third day* he rose again from the dead.'

THE END